THE LIFE AND TIMES OF
WILLIAM
SHAKESPEARE

SHAKESPEARE
HIS WORK AND WORLD

THE LIFE AND TIMES OF
WILLIAM SHAKESPEARE

EDITED BY KATHLEEN KUIPER, SENIOR EDITOR, ARTS AND CULTURE

Britannica
Educational Publishing

IN ASSOCIATION WITH

ROSEN
EDUCATIONAL SERVICES

Published in 2013 by Britannica Educational Publishing
(a trademark of Encyclopædia Britannica, Inc.)
in association with Rosen Educational Services, LLC
29 East 21st Street, New York, NY 10010.

First Edition

Britannica Educational Publishing
Adam Augustyn: Assistant Manager
J.E. Luebering: Senior Manager
Marilyn L. Barton: Senior Coordinator, Production Control
Steven Bosco: Director, Editorial Technologies
Lisa S. Braucher: Senior Producer and Data Editor
Yvette Charboneau: Senior Copy Editor
Kathy Nakamura: Manager, Media Acquisition
Kathleen Kuiper: Senior Manager, Arts and Culture

Rosen Educational Services
Jeanne Nagle: Senior Editor
Nelson Sá: Art Director
Cindy Reiman: Photography Manager
Amy Feinberg: Photo Researcher
Brian Garvey: Designer and Cover Design
Introduction by J. E. Luebering

Library of Congress Cataloging-in-Publication Data

The life and times of William Shakespeare/edited by Kathleen Kuiper.—1st ed.
    p. cm.—(Shakespeare: his work and world)
"In association with Britannica Educational Publishing, Rosen Educational Services."
Includes bibliographical references and index.
ISBN 978-1-61530-926-9 (library binding)
1. Shakespeare, William, 1564-1616. 2. Dramatists, English—Early modern, 1500-1700—
Biography. I. Kuiper, Kathleen.
PR2894.L55 2013
822.3'3—dc23
[B]
                                                                    2012019293

Manufactured in the United States of America

On the Cover: Actor Joseph Finnes, quill in hand, portraying the Bard in the 1998 film
Shakespeare in Love. Zuma Press.

Pages 1, 19, 46, 66 Hulton Archive/Getty Images

Introduction

At its most basic, the story of William Shakespeare's life is one that has been repeated countless times around the world: A young man in a small town goes to school, gets into a bit of a scrape with a woman, scurries off to a big city, becomes successful, and eventually retires, wealthy and comfortable, to the place where he began. As simple as that story is, the fact that it occurred more than 400 years ago introduces a few difficulties. Several important details of Shakespeare's life, for example, simply aren't known.

The aim of this book is to provide a description of Shakespeare's life and times. In order to do so, it weaves together the straightforward story of Shakespeare as the Warwickshire boy who struck it rich in London and a more complicated account of the attitudes and mores prevalent in Elizabethan and Jacobean society. The end result is a book that demonstrates how deeply and uniquely embedded Shakespeare was in the world he inhabited, and thus how important knowledge of his life and times is to understanding his plays and poems.

The documentary evidence of Shakespeare's life is thin, particularly by modern standards. Even something as seemingly mundane as ascertaining his birth date is problematic. Although it is almost certain that, in April 1564, someone named William Shakespeare was born in England in Stratford-upon-Avon, no documents exist that show the day on which he was born. Only a record

Statue of William Shakespeare, watching over visitors in the main reading room of the U.S. Library of Congress in Washington, D.C. Buyenlarge/Archive Photos/Getty Images

of his baptism exists, which shows that "Guliemus, filius Johannes Shakspere" was christened in Stratford on April 26, 1564. The absence of a documented birth date has, over the centuries, only encouraged a belief that Shakespeare was born on April 23, which would allow the convergence of the birth of England's greatest poet and playwright and the feast day of that country's patron saint, St. George. Whether that belief is true, however, cannot be determined.

Likewise, there is no documentary evidence of Shakespeare's education. The social standing of his family—particularly given that his father held various posts in local government, including, from 1568, a position equivalent to that of mayor—argues strongly for Shakespeare having been educated at a local, publicly funded grammar school. Essentially nothing is known for certain about what Shakespeare himself learned or experienced while in school.

In 1582, however, Shakespeare's name pops back into the historical record. In November of that year a bond was issued for a marriage license between Shakespeare and Anne Hathaway, who came from a relatively wealthy family that lived outside of Stratford. She was (likely) 26; he was 18. The probable reason for this marriage may be deduced from Shakespeare's next appearance in Stratford's records six months later, when, in May 1583, William and Anne's daughter Susanna was baptized. The couple also had twins who, records show, were baptized in February 1585.

After the last baptismal certificate, Shakespeare again vanished from official records. Just as the absence of proof of his date of birth has given rise to various beliefs, so too has the period between the mid-1580s and 1592—when the only mention of Shakespeare appears to be a written taunt by a London dramatist—encouraged speculation and outright fabrication, drawn from a variety of sources, richest of which are Shakespeare's own plays. What occupied his time during these years is simply unknown. Evidence indicates only that by 1592, Shakespeare had made his way to London, had begun working as an actor and playwright, and had been sufficiently successful as to draw the ire of at least one rival.

What is eminently clear, however, is that over the next 20 years, Shakespeare produced one of the most enduring collections of plays and poems that the world has ever known. He was closely involved during that time with a theatrical troupe called the Lord Chamberlain's Men, which featured some of the best actors of the period and inhabited the most famous theatre of its time, the Globe. Shakespeare acted with and wrote for the company, and he was a part owner of the Globe; his fortunes rose with those of the company, and he became a successful, wealthy man. Over the course of his career, he acquired properties in London and Stratford, pursued a coat of arms for his family, appeared from time to time in official records, and eventually prepared a lengthy will, in March 1616. A month later he was dead.

Does it matter that there are some holes in the documentary evidence of Shakespeare's life? Not really, because, aside from the extraordinary plays he left behind, it can be reasonably deduced that Shakespeare lived a relatively conventional middle-class life. But the times in which he lived were truly unique. About those times—which is to say, the social and cultural environment through which Shakespeare moved—we know plenty.

Shakespeare would have had his first extended contact with that world through his grammar school, the King's New School in Stratford. Although, strictly speaking, it cannot be verified that Shakespeare attended that particular school, enough is known about the school and its schoolmasters, and about others like it, that some reasonable assumptions can be made about what Shakespeare would have learned during these formative years. His early experience at school would have been heavily imbued with religion; the Book of Common Prayer, psalms, and devotional texts would have been central to the teaching of the alphabet and of reading. From there, Shakespeare would have embarked on an education centred on the Latin language and ancient Latin authors: Terence, Plautus, Cicero, Quintilian, Horace, Virgil, Ovid, Caesar, Juvenal, and more would likely have been encountered by Shakespeare in part or in full.

These texts, along with others, would have inculcated a worldview that constituted at least part of what might be called the Tudor ideal of government, as exemplified by Elizabeth I, who had begun her reign in 1558. That ideal centred on the notion of the great chain of being, in which the world was understood as an organic whole, with God above all, a divine monarch at the head of society, and each person within that society performing a specific, subordinate function. In turn, benevolent paternalism guided Elizabeth and her government in their actions. Shakespeare would have absorbed this hierarchical worldview from his reading at school, and it would have influenced his life and art.

Historical records indicate that Shakespeare did not attend university. His formal education, therefore, would have occurred solely during his time in Stratford. His plays, however, clearly show the reading Shakespeare must have done throughout his life. In addition to those Latin classics he surely encountered at King's New School, his plays show a debt in particular to Raphael Holinshed, whose second edition (1587) of *Chronicles of England, Scotland, and*

Ireland Shakespeare drew upon heavily in *Macbeth* and *King Lear*, among others. Shakespeare's plays also show the influence of contemporary playwrights, especially Christopher Marlowe, as well as other texts that reflected contemporary events, particularly exploration of the New World. Shakespeare's engagement with his world by way of texts, printed and performed throughout his career in London can thus be traced from his schooldays in Stratford.

More than texts, however, the actions of governments shaped Shakespeare's world. In 1603—after Shakespeare had been living and working in London for about a decade—the only English monarch he had known, Elizabeth, died. She was succeeded by the man who had been king of Scotland since 1567. As James I, he fashioned himself the king of Great Britain—a novel formulation that underscored the manner in which James would distinguish his reign from that of Elizabeth, who had ruled England and Ireland relatively peaceably for more than four decades. James's accession to the throne had one very narrow, concrete influence on Shakespeare: In 1603, his acting troupe's name changed, to the King's Men, when it came under James's patronage. Additionally, James's accession brought a broader, more ineffable shift, from a Tudor ideal of government to a government shaped by James's own worldview and priorities.

During his theatrical career, then, Shakespeare witnessed major shifts in political power. That he was living in London and, thus, at close proximity to the governments that wielded that power also provided him with a unique perspective on those shifts. Evidence of the manner in which Shakespeare presented contemporary political matters, implicitly and not, to a theatre-going public can be found throughout his plays. What Shakespeare the man, might have thought of Elizabeth's death or James's policies is, at best, difficult to determine. More important is the fact that Shakespeare the playwright was affected—as evidenced by his works—by the political events around him. Only by understanding those events, then, can we come to a greater understanding of his plays.

Shakespeare's career also spanned an era in which the tools he used as a dramatist—the English language and theatrical practices and conventions—were experiencing profound transformations. A look at nearly any line in the First Folio (the first collection of Shakespeare's plays, published in 1623) shows a language that appears significantly different from what readers of English today would recognize as standard modern English. And yet these differences are, typically, not enough to make the First Folio indecipherable to the modern reader. Of course, had Shakespeare looked at a manuscript written in English 400 years prior to his time, he likely would have found it unintelligible. That's because Shakespeare lived near the end of the transition from Middle English to Modern English, a period of linguistic change during which the language took on its present form—a form that Shakespeare himself, in various ways, helped to shape. The fact that printing was still a relatively new technology during Shakespeare's time also helped contribute to the sense of change and instability. The lively, imaginative approach that Shakespeare brought to the language could have thrived as it did only during the era during which he lived.

Theatrical conventions in England were in just as much flux. The later decades of the 16th century in England saw the beginnings of a shift from the ritualized, largely inexpressive "drama" of medieval morality and other religious plays to the more dynamic tragedies and comedies of the Renaissance. Of the English dramatists who fell between medieval drama and Shakespeare, the most important was Christopher Marlowe, whose engagement with the Latin classics, embrace of history as a subject for his plays, and, most important, adoption of iambic pentameter (blank verse) as the most expressive verse form for drama were crucial precedents for Shakespeare's works. One might even conjecture that his plays could not have come into being without Marlowe's.

It was therefore Shakespeare's great fortune to have lived when he did. He was someone who brought immense personal talent and savvy in the realms of art and business to a place and time uniquely suited to those talents. What resulted was a collection of plays still performed and discussed around the world today. Only by understanding the life Shakespeare lived and the world he inhabited can we fully appreciated how much, and at the same time how very little, the world and humanity have changed in four centuries.

Chapter 1

THE LIFE OF WILLIAM SHAKESPEARE

*T*he English poet, dramatist, and actor William Shakespeare is considered by many to be the greatest dramatist of all time. He occupies a position unique in world literature. Other poets, such as Homer and Dante, and novelists, such as Leo Tolstoy and Charles Dickens, have transcended national barriers as well. Yet no writer's living reputation can compare to that of Shakespeare, whose plays, written in the late 16th and early 17th centuries for a small repertory theatre, are now performed and read more often and in more countries than ever before. The prophecy of his great contemporary, the poet and dramatist Ben Jonson, that Shakespeare "was not of an age, but for all time," has been fulfilled.

It may be audacious even to attempt a definition of his greatness, but it is not so difficult to describe the gifts that enabled him to create imaginative visions of pathos and mirth that, whether read or witnessed in the theatre, fill the mind and linger there. He is a writer of great intellectual rapidity, perceptiveness, and poetic power. Other writers have had these qualities, but with Shakespeare the keenness of mind was applied not to abstruse or remote subjects but to human beings and their complete range of emotions and conflicts. Shakespeare is astonishingly clever with words and images, so that his mental energy, when applied to intelligible human situations, finds full and memorable expression, convincing and imaginatively stimulating. As if this were not enough, the art form into which most of his creative energies went, the stage play, was not remote and bookish but involved the vivid impersonation of human beings, commanding sympathy and inviting vicarious participation. Thus, Shakespeare's merits can survive translation into other languages and cultures remote from that of Elizabethan England.

Although the amount of factual knowledge available about Shakespeare is surprisingly large for one of his station in life, many find it a little disappointing, for it is mostly gleaned from documents of an official character. Dates of baptisms, marriages, deaths, and burials; wills, conveyances, legal processes, and payments by the court—these are the dusty details. There are, however, many contemporary allusions to him as a writer, and these add a reasonable amount of flesh and blood to the biographical skeleton.

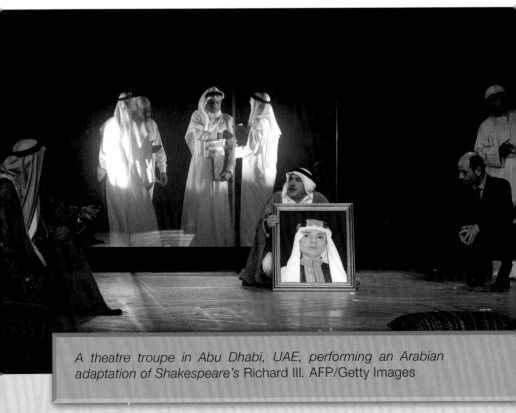

A theatre troupe in Abu Dhabi, UAE, performing an Arabian adaptation of Shakespeare's Richard III. *AFP/Getty Images*

BIRTH AND PARENTAGE

The parish register of Holy Trinity Church in Stratford-upon-Avon, Warwickshire, shows that William Shakespeare was baptized there on April 26, 1564. His birthday is traditionally celebrated on April 23. His father, John Shakespeare, was a burgess of the borough, who in 1565 was chosen an alderman and in 1568 bailiff (the position corresponding to mayor, before the grant of a further charter to Stratford in 1664). He was engaged in various kinds of trade and appears to have suffered some fluctuations in prosperity. John's wife, Mary Arden, of Wilmcote, Warwickshire, came from an ancient family and was the heiress to some land. Given the somewhat rigid social distinctions of the 16th century, this marriage must have been a step up the social scale for John Shakespeare.

EDUCATION

Shakespeare was deeply fortunate in his early education. The timing of his birth clearly played a part. It is almost certainly the case that Shakespeare's grandfather Richard Shakespeare was illiterate, and Shakespeare's father may have been as well. Neither would have had the benefit of a grammar school education.

In Shakespeare's youth, however, Stratford enjoyed a grammar school of high quality, and the education there was free, the schoolmaster's salary being paid by the borough. (School records for this period are lost, but it is very likely that the son of a prominent citizen like John Shakespeare would have been enrolled there.) Despite Ben Jonson's famous sneer at Shakespeare's "small Latine and less Greeke" in the First Folio's dedicatory poem, Shakespeare seems to have had a very substantial immersion in the standard Latin curriculum and an introduction to Greek at the excellent

Two men standing outside the cottage in Stratford-upon-Avon that is purported to be the birthplace of William Shakespeare. Frances Frith/Hulton Archive/Getty Images

King's New School in Stratford. The education was rhetorical and the language of pedagogy was Latin. Grammar school students memorized key texts, practiced translating back and forth between Latin and English, and delivered speeches in Latin. They also sometimes took part in schoolboy Latin theatricals.

The proliferation of such grammar schools throughout the 16th century is one reason that so many of the great Elizabethan playwrights—including shoemaker's son Christopher Marlowe, bricklayer's son Ben Jonson, and Shakespeare himself—were drawn from the middle ranks of English society. It was the bright, ambitious boys in such classes who gained the most from their grammar school training, even if—like Shakespeare

STRATFORD-UPON-AVON

Stratford-upon-Avon stands where a Roman road forded the River Avon; a 19th-century bridge still spans the river alongside a 15th-century arched stone bridge. The first royal charter was granted in 1553. Shakespeare was born in 1564 in a half-timbered house on Henley Street. He attended the local grammar school adjoining the medieval Chapel of the Guild of the Holy Cross.

In 1597 Shakespeare returned from London to the house known as New Place, where he died in 1616. His grave is in the parish church of Holy Trinity. It was not until 1769—more than a century and a half after the playwright's death, when the actor-producer David Garrick inaugurated the first of the annual birthday celebrations—that an attempt was made to preserve buildings and other memorials of Shakespeare's life in the town.

Today the town boasts a group of modern buildings known as the Shakespeare Centre that includes a library and art gallery (opened in 1881) and a theatre (opened in 1932). April 23—the date of Shakespeare's death and, approximately, also of his birth—is celebrated annually in Stratford-upon-Avon, and the Royal Shakespeare Company is in residence there for part of every year. The town's population at the turn of the 21st century was about 22,187.

and Jonson—they were unable to proceed to a university education at Oxford or Cambridge. It is clear from the plays that Shakespeare's imagination was a bookish one, perhaps inspired by this early education and certainly fired by his later reading. He returned to favourite books, such as Ovid's *Metamorphoses*—both in Latin and in English translation—and Sir Thomas North's English translation of Plutarch's *Parallel Lives*, over and over again for inspiration.

MARRIAGE AND FAMILY

Instead of attending university, at age 18 Shakespeare married. Where and exactly when are not known, but the episcopal registry at Worcester preserves a bond dated Nov. 28, 1582, and executed by two yeomen of Stratford, named Sandells and Richardson, as a security

This cottage in Stratford-upon-Avon was once owned by Shakespeare's wife, Anne Hathaway. It is a popular tourist destination. Travel Ink/Gallo Images/Getty Images

to the bishop for the issue of a license for the marriage of William Shakespeare and "Anne Hathaway of Stratford," upon the consent of her friends and upon once asking of the banns. (Anne died in 1623, seven years after Shakespeare. There is good evidence to associate her with a family of Hathaways who inhabited a beautiful farmhouse, now much visited, 2 miles [3.2 km] from Stratford.) The next date of interest is found in the records of the Stratford church, where a daughter, named Susanna, born to William Shakespeare, was baptized on May 26, 1583. On Feb. 2, 1585, twins were baptized, Hamnet and Judith. (Hamnet, Shakespeare's only son, died 11 years later.)

PRETHEATRE LIFE

How Shakespeare spent the next eight years or so, until his name begins to appear in London theatre records, is not known. There are stories—given currency long after his death—of stealing deer and getting into trouble with a local magnate, Sir Thomas Lucy of Charlecote, near Stratford; of earning his living as a schoolmaster in the country; of going to London and gaining entry to the world of theatre by minding the horses of theatregoers. It has also been conjectured that Shakespeare spent some time as a member of a great household and that he was a soldier, perhaps in the Low Countries. In lieu of external evidence, such extrapolations about Shakespeare's life have often been made from the internal "evidence" of his writings. But this method is unsatisfactory: one cannot conclude, for example, from his allusions to the law that Shakespeare was a lawyer, for he was clearly a writer who without difficulty could get whatever knowledge he needed for the composition of his plays.

CAREER IN THE THEATRE

The first reference to Shakespeare in the literary world of London comes in 1592, when a fellow dramatist, Robert Greene, declared in a pamphlet written on his deathbed:

> There is an upstart crow, beautified with our feathers, that with his *Tygers heart wrapt in a Players hide* supposes he is as well able to bombast out a blank verse as the best of you; and, being an absolute *Johannes Factotum*, is in his own conceit the only Shake-scene in a country.

What these words mean is difficult to determine, but clearly they are insulting, and clearly Shakespeare is the object of the sarcasms. When the book in which they appear (*Greenes, groats-worth of witte, bought with a million of Repentance*, 1592) was published after Greene's death, a mutual acquaintance wrote a preface offering an apology to Shakespeare and testifying to his worth. This preface also indicates that Shakespeare was by then making important friends. Although the puritanical city of London was generally hostile to the theatre, many of the nobility were good patrons of the drama and friends of the actors. Shakespeare seems to have attracted the attention of the young Henry Wriothesley, the 3rd earl of Southampton, and to this nobleman were dedicated his first published poems, *Venus and Adonis* and *The Rape of Lucrece*.

One striking piece of evidence that Shakespeare began to prosper early and tried to retrieve the family's fortunes and establish its gentility is the fact that a coat of arms was granted to John Shakespeare in 1596. Rough drafts of this grant have been preserved in the College of Arms, London, though the final document, which must have been handed to the Shakespeares, has not survived. Almost certainly William himself took the initiative and paid the fees. The coat of arms

Engraving of a monument to Shakespeare found in Stratford's Holy Trinity Church, where the playwright was baptized and is now buried. The top of the monument displays the Shakespeare family coat of arms. Archive Photos/Getty Images

LORD CHAMBERLAIN'S MEN

The early history of the theatrical company with which Shakespeare was intimately connected for most of his professional career as a dramatist is somewhat complicated. A company known as Hunsdon's Men, whose patron was Henry Carey, 1st Lord Hunsdon, is traceable to 1564–67. Hunsdon took office as Lord Chamberlain in 1585, and another company (the Lord Chamberlain's Men) under his patronage is traceable to 1590. Two years later the theatres closed because of plague. When they reopened in 1594, a good deal of reorganization and amalgamation between various theatre companies took place. A strong Lord Chamberlain's company emerged. After their patron's death in 1596, the company came under the protection of his son, George Carey, 2nd Lord Hunsdon. Once more it was known as Hunsdon's Men, until their new patron himself took office as Lord Chamberlain in 1597. Thereafter, it was known as the Lord Chamberlain's Men, until the accession of James I, when, by letters patent, it was taken under royal patronage and henceforth known as the King's Men.

The records of performances given at court show that they were by far the most favoured of the theatrical companies. Their only rival was a company known during Elizabeth I's reign as the Admiral's Men and after that as Prince Henry's Men. From the summer of 1594 to March 1603 the Lord Chamberlain's Men seem to have played almost continuously in London. They undertook a provincial tour during the autumn of 1597, however, and traveled again in 1603 when the plague was in London. The company went on tour during part of the summers or autumns in most years thereafter.

In 1594 their London home was for a time a theatre in Newington Butts (an archery range not far south of London Bridge) and after that most probably at the Cross Keys Inn in the city itself. Later, they presumably used The Theatre, situated in Shoreditch, which was owned by actor Richard Burbage's father. In the autumn of 1599, the company was rehoused in the Globe Theatre, built by Richard and Cuthbert Burbage on the south bank of the Thames, due west of London Bridge at Southwark. This was the company's most famous home. Profits there were shared between members of the company as such and the owners of the theatre (called "house-keepers"), who included the two Burbages, Shakespeare, and four others. Shakespeare was the company's principal dramatist (he also acted with them), but works by Ben Jonson, Thomas Dekker, and the partnership of Francis Beaumont and John Fletcher were also presented. About 1608 another theatre, in the converted monastery of the Blackfriars, became the winter headquarters of the King's Men. This was also managed by the Burbages, and profits were shared in a manner similar to that followed at the Globe.

The longest-surviving member of the original company was John Heminge, who died in 1630. The company itself ceased to exist in 1642, when the theatres were closed.

appears on Shakespeare's monument (constructed before 1623) in the Stratford church. Equally interesting as evidence of Shakespeare's worldly success was his purchase in 1597 of New Place, a large house in Stratford, which he as a boy must have passed every day in walking to school.

How his career in the theatre began is unclear, but from roughly 1594 onward he was an important member of the Lord Chamberlain's company of players (called the King's Men after the accession of James I in 1603). They had the best actor (Richard Burbage), they had the best theatre (the Globe, which was finished by the autumn of 1599), and they had the best dramatist, Shakespeare. It is no wonder that the

company prospered. Shakespeare became a full-time professional man of his own theatre, sharing in a cooperative
enterprise and intimately concerned with the financial success of the plays he wrote.

Unfortunately, written records give little indication
of the way in which Shakespeare's professional life molded
his marvelous artistry. All that can be deduced is that for 20
years Shakespeare devoted himself assiduously to his art,
writing more than a million words of poetic drama of the
highest quality.

PRIVATE LIFE

Shakespeare had little contact with officialdom, apart from
walking—dressed in the royal livery as a member of the King's
Men—at the coronation of King James I in 1604. He continued to look after his financial interests. He bought properties
in London and in Stratford. In 1605 he purchased a share
(about one-fifth) of the Stratford tithes—a fact that explains
why he was eventually buried in the chancel of its parish
church. For some time he lodged with a French Huguenot
family called Mountjoy, who lived near St. Olave's Church in
Cripplegate, London. The records of a lawsuit in May 1612,
resulting from a Mountjoy family quarrel, show Shakespeare
as giving evidence in a genial way (though unable to remem-
ber certain important facts that would have decided the case)
and as interesting himself generally in the family's affairs.

No letters written by Shakespeare have survived, but a
private letter to him happened to get caught up with some
official transactions of the town of Stratford and so has been
preserved in the borough archives. It was written by one
Richard Quiney and addressed by him from the Bell Inn in
Carter Lane, London, whither he had gone from Stratford on
business. On one side of the paper is inscribed: "To my loving
good friend and countryman, Mr. Wm. Shakespeare, deliver

these." Apparently Quiney thought his fellow Stratfordian a person to whom he could apply for the loan of £30 — a large sum in Elizabethan times. Nothing further is known about the transaction, but, because so few opportunities of seeing into Shakespeare's private life present themselves, this begging letter becomes a touching document. It is of some interest, moreover, that 18 years later Quiney's son Thomas became the husband of Judith, Shakespeare's second daughter.

Shakespeare's will (made on March 25, 1616) is a long and detailed document. It entailed his quite ample property on the male heirs of his elder daughter, Susanna. (Both his daughters were then married, one to the aforementioned

Holy Trinity Church, in which Shakespeare is interred. David Hughes/ Robert Harding World Imagery/Getty Images

Thomas Quiney and the other to John Hall, a respected physician of Stratford.) As an afterthought, he bequeathed his "second-best bed" to his wife. No one can be certain what this notorious legacy means. The testator's signatures to the will are apparently in a shaky hand. Perhaps Shakespeare was already ill.

He died in Stratford-upon-Avon on April 23, 1616. No name was inscribed on his gravestone in the chancel of the parish church there. Instead these lines, possibly his own, appeared:

> Good friend, for Jesus' sake forbear
> To dig the dust enclosed here.
> Blest be the man that spares these stones,
> And curst be he that moves my bones.

EARLY POSTHUMOUS DOCUMENTATION

Shakespeare's family or friends, however, were not content with a simple gravestone, and, within a few years, a monument was erected on the chancel wall. It seems to have existed by 1623. Its epitaph, written in Latin and inscribed immediately below the bust, attributes to Shakespeare the worldly wisdom of Nestor, the genius of Socrates, and the poetic art of Virgil. This apparently was how his contemporaries in Stratford-upon-Avon wished their fellow citizen to be remembered.

THE TRIBUTES OF HIS COLLEAGUES

The memory of Shakespeare survived long in theatrical circles, for his plays remained a major part of the repertory of the King's Men until the closing of the theatres in 1642. The greatest of Shakespeare's great contemporaries in the

Portrait of a young Ben Jonson, a contemporary of Shakespeare who, over the course of the latter's life, criticized and praised the Bard's work. Hulton Archive/ Getty Images

theatre, Ben Jonson, had a good deal to say about him. To William Drummond of Hawthornden in 1619 he said that Shakespeare "wanted art." But, when Jonson came to write his splendid poem prefixed to the Folio edition of Shakespeare's plays in 1623, he rose to the occasion with stirring words of praise:

Triumph, my Britain,
thou hast one to show
To whom all scenes of
Europe homage owe.
He was not of an age,
but for all time!

Besides almost retracting his earlier gibe about Shakespeare's lack of art, he gives testimony that Shakespeare's personality was to be felt, by those who knew him, in his poetry—that the style was the man. Jonson also reminded his readers of the strong impression the plays had made upon Queen Elizabeth I and King James I at court performances:

Sweet Swan of Avon, what a sight it were
To see thee in our waters yet appear,
And make those flights upon the banks of
Thames
That so did take Eliza and our James!

15

FIRST FOLIO

Shakespeare's collected works were first published in 1623 as *Mr. William Shakespeares Comedies, Histories & Tragedies*. This document is the major source for

contemporary texts of his plays. The publication of drama in the early 17th century was usually left to the poorer members of the Stationers' Company (which issued licenses) and to outright pirates. The would-be publisher had only to get hold of a manuscript, by fair means or foul, enter it as his copy (or dispense with the formality), and have it printed. Such a man was Thomas Thorpe, the publisher of Shakespeare's sonnets (1609). The mysterious "Mr. W.H." in the dedication is thought by some to be the person who procured him his copy.

The first Shakespeare play to be published (*Titus Andronicus*, 1594) was printed by a notorious pirate, John Danter, who also brought out, anonymously, a defective *Romeo and Juliet* (1597), largely from shorthand notes made during performance. Eighteen of Shakespeare's plays were printed in quartos (books about half the size of a modern magazine) both "good" and "bad" before the First Folio (a large-format book)

Title page of the First Folio, the first published edition (1623) of the collected works of William Shakespeare; it was originally titled Mr. William Shakespeares Comedies, Histories & Tragedies. *Photos.com/Jupiterimages*

was published. The bad quartos are defective editions, usually with badly garbled or missing text.

For the First Folio, a large undertaking of more than 900 pages, a syndicate of five men was formed, headed by the publishers Edward Blount and William Jaggard. The actors John Heminge and Henry Condell undertook the collection of 36 of Shakespeare's plays, and about 1,000 copies of the First Folio were printed, none too well, by Jaggard's son, Isaac.

In 1632 a second folio was issued and in 1663 a third. The second printing (1664) of the latter included *Pericles* (which otherwise exists only in a bad quarto) and several other plays of dubious attribution, including *The Two Noble Kinsmen* (which appeared in a quarto of 1634 and is now thought to have been a collaboration of Shakespeare and John Fletcher) and *Cardenio* (now lost), as well as *The London Prodigal* and *The History of Thomas Lord Cromwell*. In 1685 the fourth and final folio was published.

Shakespeare seems to have been on affectionate terms with his theatre colleagues. His fellow actors John Heminge and Henry Condell (who, with Burbage, were remembered in his will) dedicated the First Folio of 1623 to the earl of Pembroke and the earl of Montgomery, explaining that they had collected the plays "without ambition either of self-profit or fame; only to keep the memory of so worthy a friend and fellow alive as was our Shakespeare."

ANECDOTES AND DOCUMENTS

Seventeenth-century antiquaries began to collect anecdotes about Shakespeare, but no serious life was written until 1709, when Nicholas Rowe tried to assemble information from all available sources with the aim of producing a connected narrative. There were local traditions at Stratford: witticisms and lampoons of local characters; scandalous stories of drunkenness and sexual escapades. About 1661 the vicar of Stratford wrote in his diary: "Shakespeare, Drayton, and Ben Jonson had a merry meeting, and it seems drank too hard; for Shakespeare died of a fever there contracted." On the other hand, the antiquary John Aubrey wrote in some notes about Shakespeare: "He was not a company keeper; lived in Shoreditch; wouldn't be debauched, and, if invited to, writ he was in pain." Richard Davies, archdeacon of Lichfield, reported, "He died a papist." How much trust can be put in such a story is uncertain. In the early 18th century a story appeared that Queen Elizabeth had obliged Shakespeare "to write a play of Sir John Falstaff in love" and that he had performed the task (*The Merry Wives of Windsor*) in a fortnight. There are other stories, all of uncertain authenticity and some mere fabrications.

When serious scholarship began in the 18th century, it was too late to gain anything from traditions. But documents began to be discovered. Shakespeare's will was found in 1747 and his marriage license in 1836. The documents relating to the Mountjoy lawsuit already mentioned were found and printed in 1910. It is conceivable that further documents of a legal nature may yet be discovered, but as time passes the hope becomes more remote. Modern scholarship is more concerned to study Shakespeare in relation to his social environment, both in Stratford and in London. This is not easy, because the author and actor lived a somewhat detached life: a respected tithe-owning country gentleman in Stratford, perhaps, but a rather rootless artist in London.

Chapter 2

ELIZABETH I AND LATE TUDOR ENGLAND

S hakespeare's life bridged two eras in British history, the Tudor and Stuart. The monarchs who dominated the English world during his lifetime were Elizabeth I, who reigned until 1603, and James I (1603–25).

When Elizabeth I had taken the throne in 1558, no one would have predicted that the kingdom again stood on the threshold of an extraordinary reign. To make matters worse, she was the wrong sex. Englishmen knew that it was unholy and unnatural that "a woman should reign and have empire above men." At age 25, however, Elizabeth I was better prepared than most women to have empire over men. She had survived the palace revolutions of her brother's reign and the Roman Catholicism of her sister's; she was the product of a fine Renaissance education, and she had learned the need for strong secular leadership devoid of religious bigotry. Moreover, she possessed the magnetism of her father, Henry VIII, without his egotism or ruthlessness. She was also her mother's daughter, and the offspring of Anne Boleyn had no choice but to reestablish the royal supremacy and once again sever the ties with Rome.

Elizabeth, who was not Roman Catholic, made some religious peace by constructing a doctrine of adiaphorism, the belief that, except for a few fundamentals, there exists in religion a wide area of "things indifferent" that could be decided by the government on the basis of expediency. Conservative opposition was blunted by entitling the queen "supreme

Queen Elizabeth I in full royal regalia, including crown, sceptre, and orb. Hulton Archive/Getty Images

governor," not "head," of the church and by combining the words of the 1552 prayer book with the more conservative liturgical actions of the 1549 prayer book. At the same time, many of the old papal trappings of the church were retained. Protestant radicals went along with this compromise in the expectation that the principle of "things indifferent" meant that Elizabeth would, when the political dust had settled, rid her church of the "livery of Antichrist" and discard its "papal rags." In this they were badly mistaken, for the queen was determined to keep her religious settlement exactly as it had been negotiated in 1559. As it turned out, most of the Roman Catholic parish clergy accepted Elizabeth as supreme governor, but the Protestant radicals—the future Puritans—were soon at loggerheads with their queen.

THE TUDOR IDEAL OF GOVERNMENT

The religious settlement was part of a larger social arrangement that was authoritarian to its core. Elizabeth was determined to be queen in fact as well as in name. She tamed the House of Commons with tact combined with firmness, and she carried on a love affair with her kingdom in which womanhood, instead of being a disadvantage, became her greatest asset. The men she appointed to help her run and stage-manage the government were *politiques* like herself: William Cecil, Baron Burghley, her principal secretary and in 1572 her lord treasurer; Matthew Parker, archbishop of Canterbury; and a small group of other moderate and secular men.

THE GREAT CHAIN OF BEING

In setting her house in order, the queen followed the hierarchical assumptions of her day. All creation was presumed to be a great chain of being, running from the tiniest insect to the Godhead itself, and the universe was seen as an organic whole in which each part played a divinely prescribed role. In politics every element was expected to obey "one head, one governor, one law" in exactly the same way as all parts of the human body obeyed the brain. The crown was divine and gave leadership, but it did not exist alone, nor could it claim a monopoly of divinity, for all parts of the body politic had been created by God. The organ that spoke for the entire kingdom was not the king alone but "king in Parliament," and, when Elizabeth sat in the midst of her Lords and Commons, it was said that "every Englishman is intended to be there present from the prince to the lowest person in England."

BENEVOLENT PATERNALISM

The Tudors needed no standing army in "the French fashion" because God's will and the monarch's decrees were enshrined in acts of Parliament, and this was society's greatest defense against rebellion. The controlling mind within this mystical union of crown and Parliament belonged to the queen. The Privy Council, acting as the spokesman of royalty, planned and initiated all legislation, and Parliament was expected to turn that legislation into law. Inside and outside Parliament the goal of Tudor government was benevolent paternalism in which the strong hand of authoritarianism was masked by the careful shaping of public opinion, the artistry of pomp and ceremony, and the deliberate effort to tie the ruling elite to the crown by catering to the financial and social aspirations of the landed country gentleman.

Every aspect of government was intimate because it was small and rested on the support of probably no more than 5,000 key persons. The bureaucracy consisted of a handful of privy councillors at the top and possibly 500

Portrait of Richard Carew, the high sheriff and deputy of Cornwall in the late 1500s. The chains he is wearing were a symbol of his office. National Trust Photo Library/Art Resource, NY

paid civil servants at the bottom—the 15 members of the secretariat, the 265 clerks and custom officials of the treasury, a staff of 50 in the judiciary, and approximately 150 more scattered in other departments. Tudor government was not predominantly professional. Most of the work was done by unpaid amateurs: the sheriffs of the shires, the lord lieutenants of the counties, and, above all, the Tudor maids of all work, the 1,500 or so justices of the peace. Meanwhile, each of the 180 "corporate" towns and cities was governed by men chosen locally by a variety of means laid down in the particular royal charter each had been granted.

THE SOCIAL IDEAL

Smallness did not mean lack of government, for the 16th-century state was conceived of as an organic totality in which the possession of land carried with it duties of leadership and service to the throne, and the inferior part of society was obligated to accept the decisions of its elders and betters. The Tudors were essentially medieval in their economic and social philosophy. The aim of government was to curb competition and regulate life so as to attain an ordered and stable society in which all could share according to status. The Statute of Apprentices of 1563 embodied this concept, for it assumed the moral obligation of all men to work, the existence of divinely ordered social distinctions, and the need for the state to define and control all occupations in terms of their utility to society.

The same assumption operated in the famous Elizabethan Poor Law of 1601—the need to ensure a minimum standard of living to all men and women within an organic and noncompetitive society. By 1600 poverty, unemployment, and vagrancy had become too widespread for the church to handle, and the state had to take over,

POOR LAWS AND WORKHOUSES

Poverty in Shakespeare's time was a force to be reckoned with. A number of factors—including a huge population increase, a succession of famines, and a change in land management—had created a stability-threatening underclass of the unemployed and homeless. As a result a series of laws were passed that undertook to provide relief for the poor. They were developed in 16th-century England and maintained, with various changes, until after World War II.

An almshouse in Bristol, Eng. In Elizabethan times, those unable to work because of illness, disability, or advanced age were sent to almshouses, where they were supported by the government.
© iStockphoto.com/Amanda Lewis

The Elizabethan Poor Laws, as codified in 1597–98, were administered through parish overseers, who provided relief for the aged, sick, and infant poor, as well as work for the able-bodied. Those who were unable to work ("the lame, the impotent, the old, and the blind") were to be cared for in almshouses or "poorhouses." The idle poor and vagrants were to be sent to houses of correction. Poor children were to be made apprentices, and the able-bodied were provided for by the building of workhouses. These were to employ paupers and the indigent at profitable work. This proved difficult to do on a profitable basis, however, and workhouses showed a general tendency to degenerate into mixed receptacles where every type of pauper, whether needy or criminal, young or old, infirm, healthy, or insane, was dumped. These workhouses were difficult to distinguish from houses of correction. According to prevailing social conditions, their inmates might be let out to contractors or kept idle to prevent competition on the labour market.

instructing each parish to levy taxes to pay for poor relief and to provide work for the able-bodied, punishment for the indolent, and charity for the sick, the aged, and the disabled. The Tudor social ideal was to achieve a static class structure by guaranteeing a fixed labour supply, restricting social mobility, curbing economic freedom, and creating a kingdom in which subjects could fulfill their ultimate purpose in life—spiritual salvation, not material well-being.

ELIZABETHAN SOCIETY

Social reality, at least for the poor and powerless, was probably a far cry from the ideal, but for a few years Elizabethan England seemed to possess an extraordinary internal balance and external dynamism. In part the queen herself was responsible. She demanded no windows into men's souls,

Announcing the birth of a royal heir in a town square. In Elizabethan England, official documents and proclamations often were read aloud to the public, partly to inform the illiterate. Private Collection/ The Bridgeman Art Library

and she charmed both great and small with her artistry and tact. In part, however, the Elizabethan Age was a success because men had at their disposal new and exciting areas, both of mind and geography, into which to channel their energies.

LITERACY

A revolution in reading (and to a lesser extent writing) was taking place. By 1640 a majority of men, and just possibly a majority of men and women, could read, and there were plenty of things for them to read. In the year that Henry VIII came to the throne (1509), the number of works licensed to be published was 38. In the year of Elizabeth's accession (1558), it was 77. In the year of her death (1603), it was 328. In the year of Charles I's execution (1649), the number had risen to 1,383. And by the time of the Glorious Revolution (1688–89), it had reached 1,570.

These figures do not include the ever-rising tide of broadsheets and ballads that were intended to be posted on the walls of inns and alehouses as well as in other public places. Given that a large proportion of the illiterate population spent at least part of their lives in service in homes with literate members, and given that reading in the early modern period was frequently an aural experience—official documents being read aloud in market squares and parish churches and all manner of publications being read aloud to whole households—a very high proportion of the population had direct or indirect access to the printed word.

SCHOOLING

There was very little church building in the century after the Reformation, but there was an unprecedented growth

of school building, with grammar schools springing up in most boroughs and in many market towns. By 1600 schools were provided for more than 10 percent of the adolescent population, who were taught Latin and given an introduction to Classical civilization and the foundations of biblical faith. There was also a great expansion of university education. The number of colleges in Oxford and Cambridge doubled in the 16th century, and the number of students went up fourfold to 1,200 by 1640.

The aim of Tudor education was less to teach the "three Rs" ("reading, 'riting, and 'rithmetic") than to establish mind control: to drill children "in the knowledge of their duty toward God, their prince and all other[s] in their degree." A knowledge of Latin and a smattering of Greek became, even more than elegant clothing, the mark of the social elite. The educated Englishman was no longer a cleric but a justice of the peace or a member of Parliament, a merchant or a landed gentleman who—like Shakespeare's father—for the first time was able to express his economic, political, and religious dreams and his grievances in terms of abstract principles that were capable of galvanizing people into religious and political parties. Without literacy, the spiritual impact of the Puritans or, later, the formation of parties based on ideologies that engulfed the kingdom in civil war would have been impossible. So, too, would have been the cultural explosion that produced not only Shakespeare but the playwright Christopher Marlowe, the poets Edmund Spenser and John Donne, and the author and statesman Francis Bacon.

THE ROLE OF EXPLORATION

Poets, scholars, and playwrights dreamed and put pen to paper. Adventurers responded differently. They went "a-voyaging." From a kingdom that had once been known

Sir Walter Raleigh landing at Trinidad. Raleigh was one of several British explorers who set sail for and settled new lands during the reign of Elizabeth I. Library of Congress, Washington, D.C.

for its "sluggish security," Englishmen suddenly turned to the sea and the world that was opening up around them. The first hesitant steps had been taken under Henry VII when John Cabot in 1497 sailed in search of a northwest route to China and as a consequence discovered Cape Breton Island. The search for Cathay became an economic necessity in 1550 when the wool trade collapsed and merchants had to find new markets for their cloth. In response, the Muscovy Company was established to trade with Russia. By 1588, 100 vessels a year were visiting the Baltic. Martin Frobisher made a series of voyages to northern Canada during the 1570s in the hope of finding gold and a shortcut to Asia. John Hawkins encroached upon Spanish and Portuguese preserves and in 1562 sailed for Africa in quest of slaves to sell to West Indian plantation owners. And Sir Francis Drake circumnavigated the globe (Dec. 13, 1577–Sept. 26, 1580) in search of the riches not only of the East Indies but also of Terra Australis, the great southern continent.

Suddenly, Englishmen were on the move: Sir Humphrey Gilbert and his band of settlers set forth for Newfoundland (1583); Sir Walter Raleigh organized what became the equally ill-fated "lost colony" at Roanoke (1587–91); John Davis in his two small ships, the *Moonshine* and the *Sunshine*, reached 72° north (1585–87), the farthest north any Englishman had ever been; and the honourable East India Company was founded to organize the silk and spice trade with the Orient on a permanent basis. The outpouring was inspired not only by the urge for riches but also by religion—the desire to labour in the Lord's vineyard and to found in the wilderness a new and better nation. As it was said, Englishmen went forth "to seek new worlds for gold, for praise, for glory." Even the dangers of the reign—the precariousness of Elizabeth's throne and the struggle with Roman Catholic Spain—somehow contrived to generate a self-confidence that had been lacking under "the little Tudors."

SHAKESPEARE'S PLACE IN THE ELIZABETHAN WORLD

The relative peacefulness of 16th-century England and the long reign of Elizabeth I were crucial to time's fostering of Shakespeare. The English polity had achieved a period of genuine stability by the mid-16th century after a century of destructive feudal wars, the fractious break from the church of Rome occasioned by the divorce of Elizabeth's father, Henry VIII, and the troubled previous reigns of Elizabeth's half siblings, Edward VI and Mary I. The latter, known to subsequent ages as Bloody Mary Tudor, tried to restore England to Roman Catholicism. In the process she created many English Protestant martyrs who were burned at the stake and a lingering atmosphere of religious divisiveness. Elizabeth, returning the nation to a moderate form of Protestantism known as the Elizabethan settlement, tried unsuccessfully to quell this atmosphere of religious tension, but it lingered in the form of continued persecution and deep quarrels among Catholic recusants, radical Protestants, and more moderate Anglicans. Such religious division forced ordinary English people to choose between sharply contrasting forms of religious belief and practice. The greatest minds of the time engaged ferociously in destroying their opponents' basic religious beliefs, in demonstrating that the others' faith was based on illusion and chicanery.

Paradoxically, though, this combination of political stability and religious controversy may have been quite fortuitous for the development of Shakespeare's intellect and narrative gifts and for the great theatrical tradition of which he was a part. Albert Camus, speculating about why there have been only two ages of great tragic theatre (the theatre of Aeschylus, Sophocles, and Euripides of Athens during the 5th century BCE and the Renaissance theatre of Shakespeare and Pierre Corneille), suggested that "great periods of tragic art occur, in history, during centuries of crucial change, at moments when the lives of whole peoples are heavy both with glory and with menace, when the future is uncertain and the present dramatic." In both ages, the bare stage of the theatre represented the whole plane of human action. Hamlet is perhaps Shakespeare's most eloquent spokesman for this sense of the significance of theatre when he tells the players that the purpose of playing is to hold "the mirror up to nature" and to show "the very age and body of the time his form and pressure" and when he asks Ophelia plaintively, "What should such fellows as I do crawling between earth and heaven?"

THE ROLE OF MARY, QUEEN OF SCOTS

The first decade of Elizabeth's reign was relatively quiet, but after 1568 three interrelated matters set the stage for the crisis of the century: the queen's refusal to marry, the various plots to replace her with Mary of Scotland, and the religious and economic clash with Spain. Elizabeth Tudor's virginity was the cause of great international discussion, for every bachelor prince of Europe hoped to win a throne through marriage with Gloriana (the queen of the fairies, as she was sometimes portrayed), and was the source of even greater domestic concern, for everyone except the queen herself was convinced that Elizabeth should marry and produce heirs. The issue was the cause of her first major confrontation with the House of Commons, which was informed that royal matrimony was not a subject for commoners to discuss. Elizabeth preferred maidenhood— it was politically safer and her most useful diplomatic weapon—but it gave poignancy to the intrigues of her cousin Mary, Queen of Scots.

Mary had been an unwanted visitor-prisoner in England ever since 1568, after she had been forced to abdicate her Scottish throne in favour of her 13-month-old son, James VI (later James I). She was Henry VIII's grandniece and, in the eyes of many Roman Catholics and a number of political malcontents, the rightful ruler of England, for Mary of Scotland was a Roman Catholic. As the religious hysteria mounted, there was steady pressure put on Elizabeth to rid England of this dangerous threat, but

Portrait of Mary, Queen of Scots. The Roman Catholic Mary was found guilty of treason and executed for her role in trying to usurp the throne of her Protestant cousin, Elizabeth I. The Bridgeman Art Library/Getty Images

the queen delayed a final decision for almost 19 years. In the end, however, she had little choice. Mary played into the hands of her religious and political enemies by involving herself in a series of schemes to unseat her cousin. One plot helped to trigger the rebellion of the northern earls in 1569. Another, the Ridolfi plot of 1571, called for an invasion by Spanish troops stationed in the Netherlands and for the removal of Elizabeth from the throne and resulted in the execution in 1572 of Thomas Howard, duke of Norfolk, the ranking peer of the realm. Yet another, the Babington plot of 1586, led by Anthony Babington, allowed the queen's ministers to pressure her into agreeing to the trial and execution of Mary for high treason.

THE CLASH WITH SPAIN

Mary was executed on Feb. 8, 1587. By then England had moved from cold war to open war against Spain. Philip II was the colossus of Europe and leader of resurgent Roman Catholicism. His kingdom was strong: Spanish troops were the best in Europe, Spain itself had been carved out of territory held by the infidel and still retained its Crusading zeal, and the wealth of the New World poured into the treasury at Madrid. Spanish preeminence was directly related to the weakness of France, which, ever since the accidental death of Henry II in 1559, had been torn by factional strife and civil and religious war. In response to this diplomatic and military imbalance, English foreign policy underwent a fundamental change. By the Treaty of Blois in 1572, England gave up its historic enmity with France, accepting by implication that Spain was the greater danger.

It is difficult to say at what point a showdown between Elizabeth and her former brother-in-law

became unavoidable; there were so many areas of dis-
agreement. One of the two chief points of contention
was the refusal of English merchants-cum-buccaneers to
recognize Philip's claims to a monopoly of trade wherever the Spanish flag flew throughout the world. The
other was the military and financial support given by the
English to Philip's rebellious and heretical subjects in the
Netherlands.

The most blatant act of English poaching in
Spanish imperial waters was Sir Francis Drake's circumnavigation of the Earth, during which Spanish shipping
was looted, Spanish claims to California ignored, and
Spanish world dominion proved to be a paper empire.
But the encounter that really poisoned Anglo-Iberian
relations was the Battle of San Juan de Ulúa in September
1568, where a small fleet captained by Hawkins and
Drake was ambushed and almost annihilated through
Spanish perfidy. Only Hawkins in the *Minion* and Drake
in the *Judith* escaped. The English cried foul treachery,
but the Spanish dismissed the action as sensible tactics
when dealing with pirates. Drake and Hawkins never
forgot or forgave, and it was Hawkins who, as treasurer
of the navy, began to build the revolutionary ships that
would later destroy the old-fashioned galleons of the
Spanish Armada.

If the English never forgave Philip's treachery at San
Juan de Ulúa, the Spanish never forgot Elizabeth's inter-
ference in the Netherlands, where Dutch Protestants
were in full revolt. At first, aid had been limited to money
and the harbouring of Dutch ships in English ports, but,
after the assassination of the Protestant leader, William
I, in 1584, the position of the rebels became so desperate
that in August 1585 Elizabeth sent over an army of 6,000
under the command of Robert Dudley, earl of Leicester.
Reluctantly, Philip decided on war against England as the

Artist's rendering of Sir John Hawkins's defeat at the hands of the Spanish during the Battle of San Juan de Ulúa in 1568. Hulton Archive/Getty Images

only way of exterminating heresy and disciplining his subjects in the Netherlands. Methodically, he began to build a fleet of 130 vessels, 31,000 men, and 2,431 cannons to hold naval supremacy in the English Channel long enough for Alessandro Farnese, duke of Parma, and his army, stationed at Dunkirk, to cross over to England.

The unhappy fate of the Spanish Armada is well known, but Drake's actual role, less so. The "defeat" of the Spanish Armada was more a combination of bad weather conditions, poor planning, and old technology than anything else.

FRANCIS DRAKE AND THE SPANISH ARMADA

Francis Drake was a popular hero, but many of his great contemporaries disliked him intensely. He was the parvenu, the rich but common upstart, with none of the courtier's graces. Drake had even bought his home. It is doubtful that Drake cared about their opinions, so long as he retained the goodwill of the queen. In 1585 Elizabeth placed him in command of a fleet of 25 ships. He was ordered to cause as much damage as possible to the Spaniards' overseas empire. Drake fulfilled his commission, capturing Santiago in the Cape Verde Islands and taking and plundering the cities of Cartagena in Colombia, St. Augustine in Florida, and San Domingo (now Santo Domingo, Hispaniola).

By 1586 Elizabeth knew that Philip II was preparing a fleet for what was called "The Enterprise of England" and that he had the blessing of Pope Sixtus V to return the crown to the fold of Rome. Nothing Elizabeth could do seemed to be able to stop the Armada Catholica. Drake had been given carte blanche by the queen to "impeach the provisions of Spain." In 1587, with a fleet of some 30 ships, he showed that her trust in him had not been misplaced. He stormed into the Spanish harbour of Cádiz and in 36 hours destroyed numerous vessels and thousands of tons of supplies, all of which had been destined for the Armada. This action, which he laughingly referred to as "singeing the king of Spain's beard," succeeded only in delaying the sailing date.

That delay, however, was important, for Philip's admiral of the ocean seas, the veteran Álvaro de Bazán, marqués de Santa Cruz, died, and the job of sailing the Armada was given to Alonso Pérez de Guzmán, duque de Medina-Sidonia, who was invariably seasick and confessed that he knew more about gardening than war. What ensued was not the new commander's fault. The Armada was technologically and numerically outclassed by an English fleet of close to 200. Worse, its strategic purpose was grounded on a fallacy: that Parma's troops could be conveyed to England. The Spanish controlled no deepwater port in the Netherlands in which the Armada's great galleons and Parma's light troop-carrying barges could rendezvous.

In the end the fleet, buffeted by gales, was dashed to pieces as it sought to escape home via the northern route around Scotland and Ireland. Of the 130 ships that had left Spain, perhaps 85 crept home, 10 were captured, sunk, or driven aground by English guns, 23 were sacrificed to wind and storm, and 12 others were "lost, fate unknown."

Thomas Howard, 1st earl of Suffolk, had been chosen as English admiral to oppose the Armada. Drake managed to appropriate a prize—a Spanish galleon disabled in an accidental collision. Although he is credited by legend with a heroic role, Drake is not known to have played any part in the fighting.

THE PRICE OF WARS

When the aggressive actions of Philip II's Armada failed during the first weeks of August 1588, the crisis of Elizabeth's reign was reached and successfully passed. There were moments of great heroism and success, as when Robert Devereux, earl of Essex, Raleigh, and Thomas Howard, earl of Suffolk, made a second descent on Cádiz in 1596, seized the city, and burned the entire West Indian treasure fleet. But the war so gloriously begun deteriorated into a costly campaign in the Netherlands and France and an endless guerrilla action in Ireland, where Philip discovered he could do to Elizabeth what she had been doing to him in the Low Countries. Even on the high seas, the days of fabulous victories were over, for the king of Spain soon learned to defend his empire and his treasure fleets. Both Drake and Hawkins died in 1596 on the same ill-conceived expedition into Spanish Caribbean waters—symbolic proof that the good old days of buccaneering were gone forever.

At home the cost of almost two decades of war (£4 million) raised havoc with the queen's finances. It forced her to sell her capital (about £800,000, or roughly one-fourth of all crown lands) and increased her dependence upon parliamentary sources of income, which rose from an annual average of £35,000 to over £112,000 a year.

The expedition to the Netherlands was not, however, the most costly component of the protracted conflict. Indeed, the privateering war against Spain more than paid for itself. The really costly war of the final years of Elizabeth's reign was in Ireland, where a major rebellion in response to the exclusion of native Catholics from government and to the exploitation of every opportunity to replace native Catholics with Protestant English planters tied down thousands of English soldiers. The rebellion was exacerbated by Spanish intervention and even by a Spanish invasion force (the element of the Armada that temporarily succeeded). This Nine Years War (1594–1603) was eventually won by the English but only with great brutality and at great expense of men and treasure.

INTERNAL DISCONTENT

The moment the international danger of the war was surmounted, domestic strife ensued. Elizabeth's financial difficulties were a symptom of a mounting political crisis that under her successors would destroy the entire Tudor system of government. The 1590s were years of depression—bad harvests, soaring prices, peasant unrest, high taxes, and increasing parliamentary criticism of the queen's economic policies and political leadership. Imperceptibly, the House of Commons was becoming the instrument through which the will of the landed classes could be heard and not an obliging organ of royal control. In Tudor political theory this was a distortion of the proper function of Parliament, which was meant to beseech and petition, never to command or initiate.

Three things, however, forced theory to make way for reality. First was the government's financial dependence on the Commons, for the organ that paid the royal piper eventually demanded that it also call the governmental tune. Second, under the Tudors, Parliament had been summoned so often and forced to legislate on such crucial matters of church and state—legitimizing and bastardizing monarchs, breaking with Rome, proclaiming the supreme headship (governorship under Elizabeth), establishing the royal succession, and legislating in areas that no Parliament had ever dared enter before—that the Commons got into the habit of being consulted. Inevitably, a different constitutional question emerged: If Parliament is asked to give authority to the crown, can it also take away that authority?

Finally, there was the growth of a vocal, politically conscious, and economically dominant gentry. The increase in the size of the House of Commons reflected the activity and importance of that class. In Henry VIII's first Parliament, there were 74 knights who sat for 37 shires and 224 burgesses who represented the chartered boroughs and towns of the kingdom. By the end of Elizabeth's reign, borough representation had been increased by 135 seats. The Commons was replacing the Lords in importance because the social element it represented had become economically and politically more important than the nobility. Should the crown's leadership falter, there existed by the end of the century an organization that was quite capable of seizing the political initiative, for as one disgruntled contemporary noted: "the foot taketh upon him the part of the head and commons is become a king." Elizabeth had sense enough to avoid a showdown with the Commons, and she retreated under parliamentary attack on the issue of her prerogative rights to grant monopolies regulating and licensing the economic life of the kingdom, but on the subject of her religious settlement she refused to budge.

By the last decade of her reign, Puritanism was on the increase. During the 1570s and '80s, "cells" had sprung up to spread God's word and rejuvenate the land, and Puritan strength was centred in exactly that segment of society that had the economic and social means to control the realm—the gentry and merchant classes. What set a Puritan off from other Protestants was the literalness with which he held to his creed, the discipline with which he watched his soul's health, the militancy of his faith, and the sense that he was somehow apart from the rest of corrupt humanity. This disciplined spiritual elite clashed with the queen over the purification of the church and the stamping out of the last vestiges of Roman Catholicism. The controversy went to the root of society: Was the purpose of life spiritual or political? Was the role of the church to serve God or the crown?

In 1576 two brothers, Paul and Peter Wentworth, led the Puritan attack in the Commons, criticizing the queen for her refusal to allow Parliament to debate religious issues. The crisis came to a head in 1586, when Puritans called for legislation to abolish the episcopacy and the Anglican prayer book. Elizabeth ordered the bills to be withdrawn, and, when Peter Wentworth raised the issue of freedom of speech in the Commons, she answered by

Drawing of the Tower of London as seen from the Thames River. Those perceived as enemies of the queen, including the Puritan leader Peter Wentworth, were often imprisoned in the Tower. Hulton Archive/Getty Images

clapping him in the Tower of London. There was emerging in England a group of religious idealists who derived their spiritual authority from a source that stood higher than the crown and who thereby violated the concept of the organic society and endangered the very existence of the Tudor paternalistic monarchy. As early as 1573 the threat had been recognized:

> At the beginning it was but a cap, a surplice, and a tippet [over which Puritans complained]; now, it is grown to bishops, archbishops, and cathedral churches, to the overthrow of the established order, and to the Queen's authority in causes ecclesiastical.

James I later reduced the problem to one of his usual bons mots—"no bishop, no king." Elizabeth's answer was less catchy but more effective. She appointed as archbishop John Whitgift, who was determined to destroy Puritanism as a politically organized sect. Whitgift was only partially successful, but the queen was correct: the moment the international crisis was over and a premium was no longer placed on loyalty, Puritans were potential security risks.

Puritans were a loyal opposition, a church within the church. Elizabethan governments never feared that there would or could be a Puritan insurrection in the way they constantly feared that there could and would be a Catholic insurrection. Perhaps 1 in 5 of the peerage, 1 in 10 of the gentry, and 1 in 50 of the population were practicing Catholics, many of them also being occasional conformists in the Anglican church to avoid the severity of the law. Absence from church made householders liable to heavy fines. Associating with priests made them liable to incarceration or death. To be a priest in England was itself treasonous. In the second half of the reign, more than 300 Catholics were tortured to death, even more than the number of Protestants burned at the stake by Mary. Some priests, especially Jesuits, did indeed preach political revolution, but many others preached a dual allegiance—to the queen in all civil matters and to Rome in matters of the soul. Most laymen were willing to follow this more moderate advice, but it did not stem the persecution or alleviate the paranoia of the Elizabethan establishment.

FADING GLORY

The final years of Gloriana's life were difficult both for the theory of Tudor kingship and for Elizabeth herself. She began to lose hold over the imaginations of her subjects, and she faced the only palace revolution of her reign when her favourite, the earl of Essex, sought to take her crown. There was still fight in the old queen, and Essex ended on the scaffold in 1601, but his angry demand could not be ignored:

> What! Cannot princes err? Cannot subjects receive wrong? Is an earthly power or authority infinite? Pardon me, pardon me, my good Lord, I can never subscribe to these principles.

When the queen died on March 24, 1603, it was as if the critics of her style of rule and her concept of government had been waiting patiently for her to step down. It was almost with relief that men looked forward to the problems of a new dynasty and a new century, as well as to a man, not a woman, upon the throne.

Chapter 3

JAMES I AND EARLY STUART TIMES

*A*t the beginning of the 17th century, England and Wales contained more than four million people. The population had nearly doubled over the previous century, and it continued to grow for another 50 years. The heaviest concentrations of population were in the southeast and along the coasts. Population increase created severe social and economic problems, not the least of which was a long-term price inflation. English society was predominantly rural, with as much as 85 percent of its people living on the land. About 800 small market towns of several hundred inhabitants facilitated local exchange, and, in contrast to most of western Europe, there were few large urban areas. Norwich and Bristol were the biggest provincial cities, with populations of around 15,000. Exeter, York, and Newcastle were important regional centres, though they each had about 10,000 inhabitants.

Only London could be ranked with the great continental cities. Its growth had outstripped even the doubling of the general population. By the beginning of the 17th century, it contained more than a quarter of a million people and by the end nearly half a million, most of them poor migrants who flocked to the capital in search of work or charity. London was the centre of government, of overseas trade and finance, and of fashion, taste, and culture. It was ruled by a merchant oligarchy, whose wealth

A broad view of the city of London in the 1600s. London was a bustling, commercial city at the dawn of the 17th century, populated by more than one-quarter of a million inhabitants. Hulton Archive/Getty Images

increased tremendously over the course of the century as international trade expanded.

CONDITIONS IN LONDON AND RURAL AREAS

London not only ruled the English mercantile world, but it also dominated the rural economy of the southeast by its insatiable demand for food and clothing. The rural economy was predominately agricultural, with mixed animal and grain husbandry practiced wherever the land allowed. The population increase, however, placed great pressure upon the resources of local communities, and efforts by landlords and tenants to raise productivity for either profit or survival were the key feature of agricultural development. Systematic efforts to grow luxury market crops like wheat, especially in the environs of London, drove many smaller tenants from the land. So, too, did the practice of enclosure, which allowed for more productive land use by large holders at the expense of their poorer neighbours. There is evidence of a rural subsistence crisis lasting throughout the first two decades of the century.

Bucolic scene of the English countryside in the 17th century. The sheep grazing in the right foreground reflect the importance of the woolen cloth industry at the time. © Image Asset Management, Ltd./SuperStock

Marginally productive land came under the plow, rural revolts became more common, and harvest failures resulted in starvation rather than hunger, both in London and in the areas remote from the grain-growing lowlands—such as North Wales and the Lake District. It was not until the middle of the century that the rural economy fully recovered and entered a period of sustained growth. A nation that could barely feed itself in 1600 was an exporter of grain by 1700.

In the northeast and southwest the harsher climate and poorer soils were more suited for sheep raising than for large-scale cereal production. The northeast and southwest were the location of the only significant manufacturing activity in England, the woolen cloth industry. Wool was spun into large cloths for export to Holland, where the highly technical finishing processes were performed before it was sold commercially. Because spinning and weaving provided employment for thousands of families, the downturn of the cloth trade at the beginning of the 17th century compounded the economic problems brought about by population increase. This situation worsened considerably after the opening of the Thirty Years' War (1618–48), as trade routes became disrupted and as new and cheaper sources of wool were developed. But the transformation of the English mercantile economy from its previous dependence upon a single commodity into a diversified entrepôt that transshipped dozens of domestic and colonial products was one of the most significant developments of the century.

RANK AND STATUS

The economic divide between rich and poor, between surplus and subsistence producers, was a principal determinant of rank and status. English society was organized hierarchically with a tightly defined ascending order of privileges and responsibilities. This hierarchy was as apparent in the family as it was in the state. In the family, as elsewhere, male domination was the rule. Husbands ruled their wives, masters their servants, parents their children. But if hierarchy was stratified, it was not ossified. Those who attained wealth could achieve status. The social hierarchy reflected gradations of wealth and responded to changes in the economic fortunes of individuals. In this sense it was more open than most European societies. Old wealth was not preferred to new, and an ancient title conferred no greater privileges than recent elevation. The humble could rise to become gentle, and the gentle could fall to become humble.

During the early 17th century a small titular peerage composed of between 75 and 100 peers formed the apex of the social structure. Their titles were hereditary, passed from father to eldest son, and they were among the wealthiest subjects of the state. Most were local magnates, inheriting vast county estates and occupying honorific positions in local government. The peerage was the military class of the nation, and in the counties peers held the

Edward Montagu, the 1st earl of Sandwich. Earls, were among the titled members of the peerage in Jacobean England. Hulton Archive/ Getty Images

office of lord lieutenant. Most were also called to serve at court, but at the beginning of the century their power was still local rather than central.

Below them were the gentry, who probably composed only about 5 percent of the rural population but who were rising in importance and prestige. The gentry were not distinguished by title, though many were knights and several hundred purchased the rank of baronet (hereditary knighthoods) after it was created in 1611. Sir Thomas Smith defined a member of the gentry as "he that can bear the port and charge of a gentleman." The gentry were expected to provide hospitality for their neighbours, treat their tenants paternally, and govern their counties. They served as deputy lieutenants, militia captains, and most important, as justices of the peace. To the justices fell the responsibility of enforcing the king's law and keeping the king's peace. They worked individually to mediate local disputes and collectively at quarter sessions to try petty crimes. As the magistracy the gentry were the backbone of county governance, and they maintained a fierce local independence even while enforcing the edicts of the crown.

Beneath the gentry were those who laboured for their survival. There were many prosperous tenants who were styled yeomen to denote their economic independence and the social gulf between them and those who eked out a bare existence. Some were the younger sons of gentlemen. Others aspired to enter the ranks of the gentry, having amassed sufficient wealth to be secure against the fluctuations of the early modern economy. Like the gentry, the yeomanry were involved in local government, performing most of the day-to-day, face-to-face tasks. Yeomen were village elders, constables, and tax collectors, and they composed the juries that heard cases at quarter sessions. Most owned sufficient freehold land to be politically enfranchised and to participate in parliamentary selections.

Filling out the ranks of rural society were husbandmen, cottagers, and labourers. Husbandmen were tenant farmers at or near self-sufficiency. Cottagers were tenants with cottages and scraps of land, dependent on a range of by-employments to make ends meet ("an economy of makeshifts"). And labourers were those who were entirely dependent on waged employment on the land of others. They were the vast majority of local inhabitants, and their lives were bound up in the struggle for survival.

In towns, tradesmen and shopkeepers occupied the ranks below the ruling elites, but their occupational status clearly separated them from artisans, apprentices, and labourers. They were called the middling sort and were active in both civic and church affairs, holding the same minor offices as yeomen or husbandmen. Because of the greater concentrations of wealth and educational

Artist's depiction of a 17th-century cooper (barrelmaker) carrying the tools of his trade through the streets of his town. Tradesmen such as these, deemed roughly the equivalent of today's middle class, were frequently involved in community affairs. Science & Society Picture Library/Getty Images

opportunities, the urban middling sort were active participants in urban politics.

GOVERNMENT AND SOCIETY

Seventeenth-century government was inextricably bound together with the social hierarchy that dominated local communities. Rank, status, and reputation were the criteria that enabled members of the local elite to serve the crown either in the counties or at court. Political theory stressed hierarchy, patriarchy, and deference in describing the natural order of English society. Most of the aristocracy and gentry were the king's own tenants, whose obligations to him included military service, taxes, and local office holding. The monarch's claim to be God's vice-regent on earth was relatively uncontroversial, especially since his obligations to God included good governance. Except in dire emergency, the monarch could not abridge the laws and customs of England nor seize the persons or property of his subjects.

The monarch ruled personally, and the permanent institutions of government were constantly being reshaped. Around the king was the court, a floating body of royal servants, officeholders, and place seekers. Personal service to the king was considered a social honour and thus fitting to those who already enjoyed rank and privilege. Most of the aristocracy and many gentlemen were in constant attendance at court, some with lucrative offices to defray their expenses, others extravagantly running through their fortunes. There was no essential preparation for royal service, no necessary skills or experiences. Commonly, members of the elite were educated at universities and the law courts, and most made a grand tour of Europe, where they studied languages and culture. But their entry into royal service was normally through the patronage of family members and connections rather than through ability.

From among his court the monarch chose the Privy Council. Its size and composition remained fluid, but it was largely composed of the chief officers of state: the lord treasurer, who oversaw revenue; the lord chancellor, who was the crown's chief legal officer; and the lord chamberlain, who was in charge of the king's household. The archbishop of Canterbury was the leading

George Abbot, archbishop of Canterbury under King James I. The archbishop was part of the royal Privy Council, advising the king on matters concerning the church. Hulton Archive/Getty Images

churchman of the realm, and he advised the king, who was the head of the established church. The Privy Council advised the king on foreign and domestic policy and was charged with the administration of government. It communicated with the host of unpaid local officials who governed in the communities, ordering the justices to enforce statutes or the deputy lieutenants to raise forces. In these tasks the privy councillors relied not only upon the king's warrant but upon their own local power and prestige as well. Thus, while the king was free to choose his own councillors, he was constrained to pick those who were capable of commanding respect. The advice that he received at the council table was from men who kept one eye on their localities and the other on the needs of central policy.

This interconnection between the centre and the localities was also seen in the composition of Parliament. Parliament was another of the king's councils, though its role in government was less well defined than the Privy Council's and its summoning was intermittent. In the early 17th century, Parliament was less an institution than an event. It was convened when the king sought the aid of his subjects in the process of creating new laws or to provide extraordinary revenue. Like everything else in English society, Parliament was constituted in a hierarchy, composed of the king, Lords, and Commons. Every peer of the realm was personally summoned to sit in the House of Lords, which was dominated by the greatest of the king's officers. The lower house was composed of representatives selected from the counties and boroughs of the nation. The House of Commons was growing as local communities petitioned for the right to be represented in Parliament and local gentry scrambled for the prestige of being chosen. It had 464 members in 1604 and 507 forty years later. Selection to the House of Commons was a mark of distinction, and many communities rotated the honour among their most important citizens and neighbours. Although there were elaborate regulations governing who could choose and who could be chosen, in fact very few members of the House of Commons were selected competitively. Contests for places were uncommon, and elections in which individual votes were cast were extremely rare.

Members of Parliament served the dual function of representing the views of the localities to the king and of representing the views of the king to the localities. Most were members of royal government, either at court or in their local communities, and nearly all had responsibility for enforcing the laws that were created at Westminster. Most Parliaments were summoned to provide revenue in times of emergency, usually for defense, and most members were willing to provide it within appropriate limits. They came to Parliament to do the king's business, the business of their communities, and their own personal business in London. Such conflicting obligations were not always easily resolved, but Parliament was not perceived as an institution in opposition to the king any more than the stomach was seen as opposing the head of the body. There were upsets, however, and, increasingly during the 17th century, king and Parliament clashed over specific issues, but until the middle of the century they were part of one system of royal government.

THE ACCESSION OF JAMES I

James VI, king of Scotland (1567–1625), was the most experienced monarch to accede to the English throne since William the Conqueror, as well as one of the greatest of all Scottish kings. A model of the philosopher prince, James wrote political treatises such as *The*

James I, in a portrait dating from 1621. Photos.com/Jupiterimages

Trew Law of a Free Monarchy (1598), debated theology with learned divines, and reflected continually on the art of statecraft. He governed his poor by balancing its factions of clans and by restraining the enthusiastic leaders of its Presbyterian church. In Scotland, James was described as pleasing to look at and pleasing to hear. He was sober in habit, enjoyed vigorous exercise, and doted on his Danish wife, Anne, who had borne him two male heirs.

But James I was viewed with suspicion by his new subjects. Centuries of hostility between the two nations had created deep enmities, and these could be seen in English descriptions of the king. In them he was characterized as hunchbacked and ugly, with a tongue too large for his mouth and a speech impediment that obscured his words. It was said that he drank to excess and spewed upon his filthy clothing. It was also rumoured that he was homosexual and that he took advantage of the young boys brought to service at court. This caricature, which has long dominated the popular view of James I, was largely the work of disappointed English office seekers whose pique clouded their observations and the judgments of generations of historians.

In fact, James showed his abilities from the first. In the counties through which he passed on his way to London, he lavished royal bounty upon the elites who had been starved for honours during Elizabeth's parsimonious reign. He knighted hundreds as he went, enjoying the bountiful entertainments that formed such a contrast with his indigent homeland. He would never forget these first encounters with his English subjects, "their eyes flaming nothing but sparkles of affection." On his progress James also received a petition, putatively signed by a thousand ministers, calling his attention to the unfinished business of church reform.

TRIPLE MONARCHY

James had one overriding ambition: to create a single unified monarchy out of the congeries of territories he now found himself ruling. He wanted a union not only of the crown but of the kingdoms. He made it plain to his first Parliament that he wanted a single name for this new single kingdom; he wanted to be king not of England, Scotland, and Ireland but of Great Britain, and that is what he put on his seals and on his coins. He wanted common citizenship, the end of trade barriers, and gradual movement toward a

Coin bearing the image of King James I. text encircling the coin identifies James king of Great Britain—his name for the sin unified kingdom of scattered territories he ru © Hoberman Collection/SuperStock

union of laws, of institutions, and of churches, although he knew this could not be achieved overnight. The chauvinism of too many English elite, however, meant he was not to achieve all of his goals. A common coinage, a common flag, the abolition of hostile laws, and a joint Anglo-Scottish plantation of Ulster were all he was able to manage. Even free trade between the kingdoms was prevented by the amateur lawyers in the English House of Commons.

Having failed to promote union by legislation, he tried to promote it by stealth, creating a pan-British court and royal household, elevating Scots to the English peerage and Englishmen to the Scottish and Irish peerage, rewarding those who intermarried across borders, and seeking to remove from each of the churches those features objectionable to members of the other national churches. Progress was negligible and, under his son Charles I, went into reverse.

RELIGIOUS POLICY

The Millenary Petition (1603) initiated a debate over the religious establishment that James intended to defend. The king called a number of his leading bishops to hold a formal disputation with the reformers. The Hampton Court Conference (1604) saw the king in his element. He took a personal role in the debate and made clear that he hoped to find a place in his church for moderates of all stripes. It was only extremists that he intended to "harry from the land," those who, unlike the supporters of the Millenary Petition, sought to tear down the established church. The king responded favourably to the call for creating a better-educated and better-paid clergy and referred several doctrinal matters to the consideration of convocation. But only a few of the points raised by the petitioners found their way into the revised canons of 1604. In fact, the most important result of the conference was the establishment of a commission to provide an authorized English translation of the Bible, the King James Version (1611).

Indeed, James's hope was that moderates of all persuasions, Roman Catholic and Protestant alike, might dwell together in his church. He offered to preside at a general council of all the Christian churches—Catholic and Protestant—to seek a general reconciliation. Liberals in all churches took his offer seriously. He sought to find a formula for suspending or ameliorating the laws against Catholics if they would take a binding oath of political

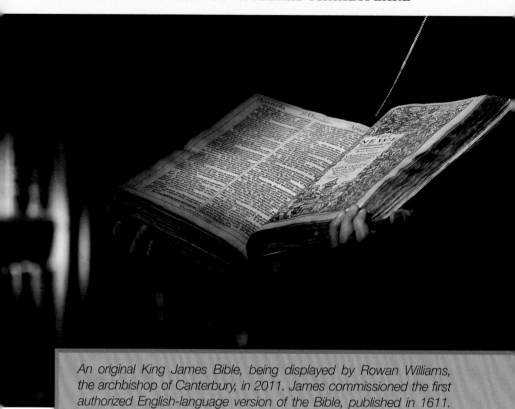

An original *King James Bible*, being displayed by Rowan Williams, the archbishop of Canterbury, in 2011. James commissioned the first authorized English-language version of the Bible, published in 1611. Matthew Lloyd/Getty Images

obedience. Most Catholics were attracted by the offer, but James's plans took a tremendous knock when an unrepresentative group of Catholics, disappointed that this son of a Catholic queen had not immediately restored Catholic liberties, plotted to kill him, his family, and his leading supporters by blowing up the Houses of Parliament in the course of a state opening, using gunpowder secreted in a cellar immediately beneath the House of Lords. The failure of the Gunpowder Plot (1605) led to reprisals against Catholics and prevented James from going any further than exhibiting humane leniency toward them in the later years of his reign. Nevertheless, James's ecumenical outlook did much to defuse religious conflict and led to 20 years of relative peace within the English church.

PURITANS

"I will make them conform or I will harry them out of the land." This was the threat that King James I of England made to the Puritans when they asked him to "purify" the state church of England of certain ceremonies and usages derived from the Roman Catholic Church, which they disliked. These Puritans were not dangerous revolutionists but plain citizens of England—farmers, merchants, professional men, and scholars—especially from the University of Cambridge. They came to be regarded as gloomy fanatics, and it was humorously said that "they objected to bear baiting, not because of the pain to the bear, but because of the pleasure to the spectators." The Puritans were not precisely that, however. The writings of one of the foremost Puritans, John Milton, have come down as a priceless literary heritage.

Puritans (right) beseeching James I to reform the Church of England. Hulton Archive/Getty Images

The Puritans were the advanced wing of the Protestants in England in the days of the Reformation. The division began among the religious exiles from England who sought refuge on the Continent during the Roman Catholic persecutions of Queen Mary's reign. It became acute at Frankfurt am Main, Germany, in the quarrels between the Knoxians and Coxians (followers of John Knox and Dr. Richard Cox) over the wearing of priestly vestments. In general the Puritans inclined to follow the lead of Knox, Calvin, and the Swiss reformers, who would reject all usages of the Roman church for which positive warrant was not found in the Scriptures. They would thus reduce the worship in their churches to the bare simplicity of apostolic times. So arose their opposition to written prayers, religious images and pictures in churches, instrumental music at services, and the like.

Some of the Puritans, instead of wanting merely to purify the church services, wanted to change the whole government of it as well. The Presbyterians, for instance, wanted to do away with the government of bishops in the church but would retain a state church. Others, called Separatists, or Independents, wanted the church and state to be entirely separated and each congregation to manage its own affairs. These were later called Congregationalists. Still more radical reformers called Anabaptists thought baptism by immersion should be only for adults and held other unconventional views as to church and state.

It was a band of the Separatists who went first to Holland in 1608 and then to America in 1620, where they founded Plymouth Colony. Thousands of others went to America, especially during the Great Migration of 1630–40. When the English Civil War gave the Puritans control of the government, the emigration stopped for a time.

SHAKESPEARE'S RELIGIOUS VIEWS

Shakespeare's own religious views cannot be known with certainty. But his plays suggest a deep interest in the efficacy of ritual and the status of symbolic language, matters clearly related to theatre as a representational art. In Shakespeare's day, performance of public plays required state licensing—the express permission of a court officer known as the Master of the Revels—and punishment for violating theatrical censorship could be severe. Such censorship, it has been argued by such scholars as Annabel Patterson, is a powerful stimulus to developing "a system of communication in which ambiguity becomes a creative and necessary instrument, a social and cultural force of considerable consequence." Shakespeare became a master of such ambiguity, and, if his plays encode topical allusions to religious controversy, as scholars have sometimes argued, they do so without sacrificing their purchase on timelessness.

Chapter 4

THE ENGLISH LANGUAGE AND THE THEATRE IN SHAKESPEARE'S TIME

A full picture of the context in which Shakespeare created his enduring plays and poetry can be rounded out with two further considerations. These are the state of the English language when it became the Bard's primary medium and the state of English theatre when he took a notion to try his hand at performing and writing.

ENGLISH IN SHAKESPEARE'S TIME

Modern Icelanders can still read and understand Old Icelandic sagas without difficulty. The same is not true for modern speakers of English. Old English—the language of Caedmon (the first Old English poet) and of the heroic poem *Beowulf*—is not understandable, much less pronounceable, by anyone who has not studied the language at some length. The English used by Shakespeare cannot be appreciated without an understanding of its evolution from what is today an arcane language.

OLD ENGLISH TO MIDDLE ENGLISH

With the Norman Conquest of 1066—the military conquest of England by William, duke of Normandy—the English language began its first major shift, from what is known as Old English to Middle English. The result was the placement of all four Old English dialects more or less on one level. West Saxon lost its supremacy, and the centre of culture and learning gradually shifted from Winchester to London. The old Northumbrian dialect became divided into Scottish and Northern, although little is known of either of these divisions before the end of the 13th century. The old Mercian dialect was split into East and West Midland. West Saxon became slightly diminished in area and was more appropriately named the South Western dialect. The Kentish dialect was considerably extended and was called South Eastern accordingly. All five Middle English dialects (Northern, West Midland, East Midland, South Western, and South Eastern) went their own ways and developed their own characteristics. The so-called Katherine Group of writings (1180–1210), associated with Hereford, a town not far from the Welsh border, adhered most closely to native traditions, and there is something to be said for regarding this West Midland dialect, least disturbed by French and Scandinavian intrusions, as a kind of Standard English in the High Middle Ages.

Another outcome of the Norman Conquest was to change the writing of English from the clear and easily readable insular hand of Irish origin to the delicate Carolingian script then in use on the Continent. With the change in appearance came a change in spelling. Norman scribes wrote Old English *y* as *u*, *ȳ* as *ui*, *ū* as *ou* (*ow* when final). Thus, *mycel* ("much") appeared as *muchel*, *fȳr* ("fire") as *fuir*, *hūs* ("house") as *hous*, and *hū* ("how") as *how*. For the sake of clarity (i.e., legibility) *u* was often written *o* before and after *m, n, u, v,* and *w*; and *i* was sometimes written *y* before and after *m* and *n*. So *sunu* ("son") appeared as *sone* and *him* ("him") as *hym*. Old English *cw* was changed to *qu*; *hw* to *wh, qu,* or *quh*; *ċ* to *ch* or *tch*; *sċ* to *sh*; *-ċg-* to *-gg-*; and *-ht* to *ght*. So Old English *cwēn* appeared as *queen*; *hwaet* as *what, quat,* or *quhat*; *dīċ* as *ditch*; *sċip* as *ship*; *secge* as *segge*; and *miht* as *might*.

Bible written in Carolingian script. The Norman Conquest brought about several language reforms, including the written style and spellings of English words. SuperStock/Getty Images

For the first century after the Norman Conquest, most loanwords came from Normandy and Picardy, but with the extension south to the Pyrenees of the Angevin empire

of Henry II (reigned 1154–89), other dialects, especially Central French, or Francien, contributed to the speech of the aristocracy. As a result, Modern English acquired the forms *canal, catch, leal, real, reward, wage, warden,* and *warrant* from Norman French side by side with the corresponding forms *channel, chase, loyal, royal, regard, gage, guardian,* and *guarantee,* from Francien. King John lost Normandy in 1204. With the increasing power of the Capetian kings of Paris, Francien gradually predominated. Meanwhile, Latin stood intact as the language of learning. For three centuries, therefore, the literature of England was trilingual. *Ancrene Riwle,* for instance, a guide or rule (*riwle*) of rare quality for recluses or anchorites (*ancren*), was disseminated in all three languages.

The sounds of the native speech changed slowly. Even in late Old English short vowels had been lengthened before *ld, rd, mb*, and *nd*, and long vowels had been short-ened before all other consonant groups and before double consonants. In early Middle English short vowels of what-ever origin were lengthened in the open stressed syllables of disyllabic words. An open syllable is one ending in a vowel. Both syllables in Old English *nama* "name," *mete* "meat, food," *nosu* "nose," *wicu* "week," and *duru* "door" were short, and the first syllables, being stressed, were lengthened to *nāme, mēte, nōse, wēke*, and *dōre* in the 13th and 14th centuries. A similar change occurred in 4th-century Latin, in 13th-century German, and at different times in other languages. The popular notion has arisen that final mute -*e* in English makes a preceding vowel long. In fact, however, it is the lengthening of the vowel that has caused *e* to be lost in pronunciation. On the other hand, Old English long vowels were shortened in the first syl-lables of trisyllabic words, even when those syllables were open; e.g., *hāligdaeg* "holy day," *ærende* "message, errand," *crīstendōm* "Christianity," and *sūtherne* "southern" became *hŏliday* (Northern *hăliday*), *ĕrrende, chrĭstendom*, and *sūtherne*. This principle still operates in current English. Compare, for example, trisyllabic derivatives such as the words *chastity, criminal, fabulous, gradual, gravity, linear, national, ominous, sanity,* and *tabulate* with the simple nouns and adjectives *chaste, crime, fable, grade, grave, line, nation, omen, sane,* and *table*.

There were significant variations in verb inflections in the Northern, Midland, and Southern dialects. The Northern infinitive was already one syllable (*sing* rather than the Old English *singan*), whereas the past participle -*en* inflection of Old English was strictly kept. These appar-ently contradictory features can be attributed entirely to Scandinavian, in which the final -*n* of the infinitive was lost early in *singa*, and the final -*n* of the past parti-ciple was doubled in *sunginn*. The Northern unmutated present participle in *-and* was also of Scandinavian origin. Old English mutated *-ende* (German *-end*) in the present participle had already become *-inde* in late West Saxon, and it was this Southern *-inde* that blended with the *-ing* suffix (German *-ung*) of nouns of action that had already become near-gerunds in such compound nouns as *athswering* "oath swearing" and *writingfether* "writing feather, pen." This blending of present participle and gerund was further helped by the fact that Anglo-Norman and French *-ant* was itself a coalescence of Latin present participles in *-antem, -entem*, and Latin gerunds in *-andum, -endum*. The Northern second person singular *singis* was inherited unchanged from Common Germanic. The final *t* sound in Midland *-est* and Southern *-st* was excrescent (added without any etymological reason), comparable with the final *t* in modern *amidst* and *amongst* from older *amiddes* and *amonges*. The Northern third person singular *singis* had a quite different origin. Like the *singis* of the plural, it resulted almost casually from an inadvertent retraction of the tongue in enunciation from an interdental *-th* sound to postdental *-s*. In Modern English the form *singeth* survives as a poetic archaism. Shakespeare used both *-eth* and *-s* endings ("It [mercy] blesseth him that gives and him that takes," *The Merchant of Venice*). The Midland present plural inflection *-en* was taken from the subjunctive. The past participle prefix *y-* developed from the Old English perfective prefix *ge-*.

The author of *The Canterbury Tales*, Geoffrey Chaucer, who was born and died in London, spoke a dialect that was basically East Midland. Compared with his contemporaries, he was remarkably modern in his use of language. He was in his early 20s when the Statute of Pleading (1362) was passed, by the terms of which all court proceedings were henceforth to be conducted in English, though "enrolled in Latin." Chaucer himself used four languages. He read Latin (Classical and Medieval) and spoke French and Italian on his travels. For his own literary work he deliberately chose English.

FROM MIDDLE ENGLISH TO THE EARLY MODERN ENGLISH OF SHAKESPEARE

The death of Chaucer at the close of the century (1400) marked the beginning of the period of transition from Middle English to the Early Modern English stage. The Early Modern English period is regarded by many scholars as beginning about 1500 and terminating with the return of the monarchy (John Dryden's *Astraea Redux*) in 1660. The three outstanding developments of the 15th century were the rise of London English, the invention of printing, and the spread of the new learning.

THE RISE OF LONDON ENGLISH

Although the population of London in 1400 was only about 40,000, it was by far the largest city in England. York came second, followed by Bristol, Coventry, Plymouth, and Norwich. The Midlands and East Anglia, the most densely peopled parts of England, supplied London with streams of young immigrants. The speech of the capital was mixed, and it was changing. The seven long vowels of Chaucer's speech had already begun to shift. Incipient diphthongization of high front /i:/ (the *ee* sound in *meet*) and high back /u:/ (as in *fool*) led to instability in the other five long vowels. (Symbols within slash marks are taken from the International Phonetic Alphabet.) This remarkable event, known as the Great Vowel Shift, changed the whole vowel system of London English. As /i:/ and /u:/ became diphthongized to /ai/ (as in *bide*) and /au/ (as in *house*) respectively, so the next highest vowels, /e:/ (this sound can be heard in the first part of the diphthong in *name*) and /o:/ (a sound that can be heard in the first part of the diphthong in *home*), moved up to take their places, and so on.

When William Caxton started printing in 1476, he was painfully aware of the uncertain state of the English language. Sentence structures were being gradually modified, but many remained untidy. For the first time, nonprofessional scribes, including women, were writing at length.

BORROWED FROM THE CLASSICS

The revival of classical learning was one aspect of that Renaissance that arose in Italy and spread to France and England. It evoked a new interest in Greek on the part of learned men. John Colet, dean of St. Paul's School in the first quarter of the 16th century, startled his congregation by expounding the Pauline Epistles of the Christian New Testament as living letters. The deans who had preceded him had known no Greek because they had found in Latin all that they required. Only a few medieval churchmen could read Greek with ease. Although the names of the seven liberal arts of the medieval curricula (the trivium and the quadrivium) were all Greek—grammar, logic, and rhetoric; arithmetic, geometry, astronomy, and music—they had come into English not from the original but by way of French.

Renaissance scholars adopted a liberal attitude to language. They borrowed Latin words through French, or Latin words direct; Greek words through Latin, or Greek words direct. Latin was no longer limited to Church Latin: it embraced all Classical Latin. For a time the whole Latin lexicon became potentially

WILLIAM CAXTON

(b. *c.* 1422, Kent, England—d. 1491, London)

William Caxton, Great Britain's first printer.
Hulton Archive/Getty Images

The first English printer was William Caxton. As a translator and publisher, he exerted an important influence on English literature. In 1438 he was apprenticed to Robert Large, a rich mercer (dealer in expensive fabrics), who in the following year became lord mayor of London. Large died in 1441, and Caxton moved to Brugge (now in Belgium), the centre of the European wool trade. During the next 30 years he became an increasingly prosperous and influential member of the English trading community in Flanders and Holland. Sometime in 1470 he entered the service of Margaret, duchess of Burgundy.

In that period Caxton's interests were turning to literature. In March 1469 he had begun to translate Raoul Le Fèvre's *Recueil des histoires de Troye*, which he laid aside and did not finish until 1471. In Cologne, where he lived from 1470 to the end of 1472, he learned printing. In the epilogue of Book III of the completed translation, titled *The Recuyell of the Historyes of Troye*, he tells how his "pen became worn, his hand weary, his eye dimmed" with copying the book. As a result he "practised and learnt" at great personal cost how to print it and set up a press in Brugge about 1474. *The Recuyell*, the first book printed in English, was published there in 1475. Toward the end of 1476 he returned to England, established his press at Westminster, and devoted himself to writing and printing. The first dated book printed in English, *Dictes and Sayenges of the Phylosophers*, appeared in 1477.

Kings, nobles, and rich merchants were Caxton's patrons and sometimes commissioned special books. His varied output—including books of chivalric romance, conduct, morality, history, and philosophy and an encyclopaedia, *The Myrrour of the Worlde* (1481), the first illustrated English book—shows that he catered also to a general public. The large number of service books and devotional works published by Caxton were the staple reading of most literate persons. He also printed nearly all the English literature available to him in his time, including works by Chaucer, John Gower, and Sir Thomas Malory. The 100 or so items he published included 24 of his own translations.

English. Some words, such as *consolation* and *infidel*, could have come from either French or Latin. Others, such as the terms *abacus, arbitrator, explicit, finis, gratis, imprimis, item, memento, memorandum, neuter, simile*, and *videlicet*, were taken straight from Latin. Words that had already entered the language through French were now borrowed again, so that doublets arose: *benison* and *benediction*; *blame* and *blaspheme*; *chance* and *cadence*; *count* and

RischgitzHulton Archive/Getty Images

compute; *dainty* and *dignity*; *frail* and *fragile*; *poor* and *pauper*; *purvey* and *provide*; *ray* and *radius*; *sever* and *separate*; *strait* and *strict*; *sure* and *secure*. The Latin equivalents for *kingly* and *lawful* have even given rise to triplets: in the forms *real, royal,* and *regal* and *leal, loyal,* and *legal,* they were imported first from Anglo-Norman, then from Old French, and last from Latin direct.

ENGLISH TO THE RESTORATION

After the dawn of the 16th century, English prose moved swiftly toward modernity. In 1525 Lord Berners completed his translation of Jean Froissart's *Chronicle*, and William Tyndale translated the New Testament. One-third of the King James Bible (1611), it has been computed, is worded exactly as Tyndale left it. Between 1525 and 1611 lay the Tudor Golden Age, with its culmination in Shakespeare. Too many writers, to be sure, used "inkhorn terms" (newly coined, ephemeral words), and too many vacillated between Latin and English. Sir Thomas More actually wrote his *Utopia* in Latin. It was translated into French during his lifetime but not into English until 1551, some years after his death. Francis Bacon published *De dignitate et augmentis scientiarum (On the Dignity and Advancement of Learning*, an expansion of his earlier *Advancement of Learning)* in Latin in 1623. William Harvey announced his epoch-making discovery of the circulation of the blood in his Latin *De Motu Cordis et Sanguinis in Animalibus* (1628; *On the Motion of the Heart and Blood in Animals*). John Milton composed polemical treatises in the language of Cicero. As Oliver Cromwell's secretary, he corresponded in Latin with foreign states. His younger contemporary Sir Isaac Newton lived long enough to bridge the gap. He wrote his *Principia* (1687) in Latin but his *Opticks* (1704) in English.

SHAKESPEARE'S LANGUAGE

It is indisputable that had Shakespeare been born even a half-century earlier—in 1514 rather than 1564—he could not and would not have written his plays because they arose from specific historical conditions unique to his era. If there is no satisfactory explanation for the appearance of great genius, it is not too difficult to articulate the cultural conditions that extinguish it. Certainly it is unlikely that in 1514 the son of a Midlands tradesman would have been literate, let alone that he would have written poetry. Thus, first place among the necessary, if not sufficient, historical preconditions for the creation of Hamlet and Sir John Falstaff must go to the development of English as a serious literary language. Shakespeare's Early Modern English poses enough semantic and syntactic difficulties to require editorial annotation—that swift glance to the bottom of the page that informs us that many familiar words, such as *virtue* and *honesty* and *credit*, had different meanings then.

Most readers of Shakespeare do not realize how remarkably fortunate the poet was to come of age when English first blossomed as a great literary language. In Shakespeare's childhood, Latin was still the language of theology and science, and a peculiar form of Anglo-Norman was used in legal contexts. As was noted above, written English had not yet achieved standardization in spelling, syntax, or grammatical forms. There was no dictionary of English. By the end of the 16th century, English was ready for transformation into one of the greatest mediums for the representation of thought, emotion, and complex inner states ever created by any society.

Shakespeare played a huge role in expanding the expressive capacity of the language, especially in the verbal representation of thinking and subjectivity. But the language, written and spoken, relied on expansion through borrowing from Latin and the European vernacular tongues. Such borrowing was and continues to be a major reason for the expansiveness of English. For writers like Shakespeare, the ready absorption of foreign words must have been a powerful stimulus to stylistic and intellectual invention. The massive and relatively sudden explosion of great literary creativity during Shakespeare's lifetime supports this supposition, as does the appearance of works such as Richard Mulcaster's *The First Part of the Elementarie* (1582), which devotes itself, in part, to the defense of English as a literary tongue. Mulcaster believed that English had entered upon a formative golden age: "Such a period in the Greke tung was that time, when Demosthenes lived, and that learned race of the father philosophers: such a period in the Latin tung, was that time, when Tullie [Cicero] lived, and those of that age: such a period in the English tung I take this to be in our daies."

The defeat of the Spanish Armada and the glorification of Elizabeth I in the wake of that fortuitous event also promoted the status of English—just when Shakespeare had arrived in London and was beginning his career as an actor and playwright. One scholar speculates that even Shakespeare's Midland origins facilitated his personal creation of a comparatively "richer linguistic palate." A writer born near London would have heard a more modern form of English in his linguistically formative early years than the rich mixture of older and newer forms that would have surrounded a Warwickshire youth. Hearing such variation and change may have stimulated Shakespeare's consciousness of language and a desire to play with it. Perhaps this is also why Shakespeare's colleague and great rival, the

London-born Ben Jonson, establishes himself instead as a linguistic purist and rule setter—specifying in the prologue to his *Every Man in His Humour* that the material of comedy be "deeds, and language, such as men do use."

Shakespeare, by contrast, seems to revel in polyglot wordplay and neologism, allowing the intensely guilt-ridden Macbeth, for example, to worry that he can never wash off the murdered Duncan's blood, that "this my hand will rather / The multitudinous seas incarnadine, making the green one red." Shakespeare's use of this hyperbolic image of a murderer's bloody hand staining the ocean is not new. There are numerous Classical antecedents. What is new in Shakespeare is his use of a massively polysyllabic monologue using two new Latinate words—*multitudinous* and *incarnadine*—that he may well have invented.

THEATRE IN ENGLAND

The influence of the Italian Renaissance was relatively weak in England, but the theatre of the Elizabethan Age was all the stronger for it. Apart from the rediscovery of Classical culture, the 16th century in England was a time for developing a new sense of national identity, necessitated by the establishment of a national church. Furthermore, because the English were more suspicious of Rome and the Latin tradition, there was less imitation of Classical dramatic forms and an almost complete disregard for the rules that bound the theatre in France and Italy. England built on its own foundations by adapting the strong native tradition of medieval religious drama to serve a more secular purpose. When some of the Continental innovations were blended with this cruder indigenous strain, a rich synthesis was produced. Consequently, the theatre that emerged was resonant, varied, and in touch with all segments of society. It included the high seriousness of morality plays, the sweep of chronicle histories, the fantasy of romantic comedies, and the irreverent fun of the interludes.

At the same time, the English theatre had to contend with severe restrictions. The suppression of the festival of Corpus Christi in 1548 as a means of reinforcing the Protestant church marked the rapid decline of morality plays and mystery cycles. Their forced descent into satirical propaganda mocking the Roman Catholic faith polarized the audience and led to riots. By 1590 playwrights were prohibited from dramatizing religious issues and had to resort to history, mythology, allegory, or allusion in order to say anything about contemporary society. Flouting these restrictions meant imprisonment. Nevertheless, playwrights managed to argue highly explosive political topics. In William Shakespeare's histories, for instance, the subject of kingship is thoroughly examined in all its implications: both the rightful but incompetent sovereign and the usurping but strong monarch are scrutinized—a most daring undertaking during the reign of Elizabeth I.

The situation for actors was not helped by the hostile attitude of the City of London authorities, who regarded theatre as an immoral pastime to be discouraged rather than tolerated. Professional companies, however, were invited to perform at court from the beginning of the 16th century (though on a smaller scale than on the Continent), and public performances took place wherever a suitable space could be found—in large rooms of inns, in halls, or in quiet innyards enclosed on all sides with a temporary platform stage around which spectators could gather while others looked out from the windows above. But such makeshift conditions only stalled the development of the drama and kept it on an amateurish level.

FEAST OF CORPUS CHRISTI

The Feast of Corpus Christi is a festival of the Latin rite church in honour of the Real Presence of the body (*corpus*) and blood of Jesus Christ in the sacrament called the Eucharist, or Lord's Supper. A movable observance, it is observed on the Thursday (or, in some countries, the Sunday) after Trinity Sunday. It originated in 1246 when Robert de Torote, bishop of Liège, ordered the festival celebrated in his diocese. He was persuaded to initiate the feast by Blessed Juliana, prioress of Mont Cornillon near Liège (1222–58), who had experienced a vision. It did not spread until 1261, when Jacques Pantaléon, formerly archdeacon of Liège, became pope as Urban IV. In 1264 he ordered the whole church to observe the feast. Urban's order was confirmed by Pope Clement V at the Council of Vienne in 1311–12. By the mid-14th century the festival was generally accepted, and in the 15th century it became, in effect, the principal feast of the church.

The procession became the feast's most prominent feature and was a pageant in which sovereigns and princes took part, as well as magistrates and members of guilds. In the 15th century the procession was customarily followed by the performance by guild members of miracle plays and mystery plays.

After the doctrine of transubstantiation was rejected during the Reformation, the festival was suppressed in Protestant churches.

ELIZABETHAN THEATRE

These conditions improved considerably in 1574, when regular weekday performances were legitimized, and in 1576, when the first playhouse, called simply The Theatre, was built by James Burbage. It was erected in London

immediately outside the city boundary. Others followed, including the Curtain, the Rose, the Swan, and the Globe, where most of Shakespeare's plays were first staged.

Just as the Spanish playhouse reproduced the features of the *corrale* it had grown out of, so the Elizabethan playhouse followed the pattern of the improvised innyard theatre. It was an enclosed circular structure containing two or three galleries with benches or stools. Spectators could also stand in an unroofed space on three sides of the raised platform stage, which extended into the middle of the theatre. Behind the stage was a wall with curtained doors and, above this, an actors' and musicians' gallery. Large numbers of people could be accommodated, and the price was kept low at between one penny and sixpence. This type of stage allowed for fluid movement and considerable intimacy between actors and audience, while its lack of scenery placed the emphasis firmly on the actor interpreting the playwright's words. Such sheer simplicity presented a superb challenge for the writer; the quality of both language and acting had to be good enough to hold the attention of the spectators and make them use their imaginations.

This challenge was quickly taken up by a generation of playwrights who could carry forward the established dramatic forms and test the possibilities of the new stage. Christopher Marlowe was the major innovator, developing a vigorous style of tragedy that was refined by Shakespeare, who began writing for the theatre about 1590. At this time, professional companies operated under the patronage of a member of the nobility. In Shakespeare's company, known as the Chamberlain's Men (later renamed the King's Men), the actors owned their playhouse, prompt books, costumes, and properties, and they shared in the profits. Other companies paid rent to the patron, who paid their salaries. There were very few rehearsals for a new play, and

An audience watching a show at the reconstructed Globe Theatre. The building's circular configuration, multi tiered seating, and accessible platform stage were typical features of Elizabethan theatres. Andrea Pistolesi/The Image Bank/Getty Images

because the texts were not immediately printed (to avoid pirating by rival companies) each actor was usually given only his own lines, with the relevant cues, in manuscript form. No women appeared on the Elizabethan stage. Female roles were taken either by boy actors or, in the case of older women, by adult male comedians. (This performance practice was famously followed by British actor

and director Mark Rylance, who was associated with the reconstructed Globe Theatre at the turn of the 21st century.) As in Italy, all the actors had to be able to sing and dance and often to generate their own music. The great actors of the day were Richard Burbage, who worked in Shakespeare's company, and Edward Alleyn, who was mainly associated with Ben Jonson. In spite of the fact that theatres such as the Globe played to a cross section of London's populace, audiences seem to have been attentive and well behaved.

An alternative to the outdoor public playhouse was the private indoor theatre. The first of these was an abandoned monastery near St. Paul's Cathedral, converted in 1576 by Richard Farrant and renamed the Blackfriars Theatre. Others included the Cockpit, the Salisbury Court, and the Whitefriars. Initially these theatres were closer to the Spanish model, with a bare stage across one end, an inner stage at the back, benches in front for the audience, and galleries all around. Later, they made use of more elaborate scenery and featured the Italian-style proscenium arch. Because of the reduced size of the audience in such a setup, higher prices had to be charged, which excluded all but the more wealthy and learned segment of the public. This, in turn, affected the style of writing. These private theatres were mostly used by children's, or boys', companies that presented a more refined and artificial type of drama. One of their chief dramatists was John Lyly, though Ben Jonson wrote many of his plays for them. Growing rivalry between the boy and adult companies, exacerbated by hostility from the increasingly powerful

CHILDREN'S COMPANIES

The young male actors who formed children's, or boys', companies (troupes for the performance of plays) were drawn primarily from choir schools attached to the great chapels and cathedrals, where they received musical training and were taught to perform in religious dramas and classical Latin plays. By the time of Henry VIII, groups such as the Children of the Chapel and the Children of Paul's were often called upon to present plays and to take part in ceremonies and pageants at court. During the reign of Queen Elizabeth I, these groups were formed into highly professional companies, usually consisting of 8 to 12 boys, who gave public performances outside the court. The choirmasters of the companies functioned as managers, directors, writers of music and plays, and designers of masques and pageants, in addition to performing their regular duties of training the boys to sing and act.

In the late 16th and early 17th centuries, these companies were so popular that they posed a serious threat to the professional men's companies. Shakespeare has Hamlet refer scornfully to the child actors as "little eyases," or nestling birds, that "are now the fashion." Children acted in the first Blackfriars Theatre (c. 1576–80), and in 1600 a syndicate representing the Children of the Chapel acquired a lease on the second Blackfriars Theatre, where the boys performed many important plays, including those of John Marston and Ben Jonson. By roughly 1610 the children's companies had greatly declined in popularity, aided perhaps by the companies' indulgence in political criticism.

Puritan movement, resulted in James I imposing even tighter controls and exercising heavy censorship on the theatre when he came to the throne in 1603.

JACOBEAN THEATRE

Although the Italian influence gradually became stronger in the early part of the 17th century, the English theatre was by then established and confident enough to take over foreign ideas without losing any of its individuality. Shakespeare had made an indelible mark on the development of the English theatre. Ben Jonson became increasingly preoccupied with the dramatic unities, while other writers of the Jacobean period such as John Webster, Thomas Middleton, and John Ford favoured a more definite separation of comedy and tragedy than had been the case in Elizabethan drama. They were given to sensationalism in their revenge plays, finding inspiration in Spanish cloak-and-sword drama and in the darker moods of Seneca and often setting their own plays in Italy.

Meanwhile, at court the pastoral was finding new popularity, partly because it provided opportunities for spectacular scenery, and with it came the revival of the masque—an allegorical entertainment combining poetry, music, dance, scenery, and extravagant costumes. As court poet, Ben Jonson collaborated with the architect and designer Inigo Jones to produce some of the finest examples of the masque. But ultimately Jonson saw that the visual elements were completely overtaking the dramatic content. When the Civil War broke out in 1642, the Puritans closed all the theatres and forbade public dramatic performances of any kind. When after 18 years the theatre began to flourish once more, it was along quite different lines.

SHAKESPEARE AND THE THEATRE

An examination of Shakespeare's social, artistic, and linguistic context makes it clear, then, that good timing was

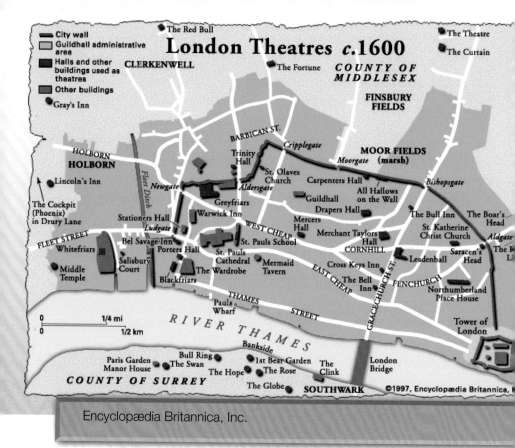

Encyclopædia Britannica, Inc.

involved in the arrival of William Shakespeare in London
sometime in the late 1580s, when public theatrical performance by professional actors in purpose-built playhouses
was an emerging commercial enterprise looking for talent
and as hungry for content as today's cable TV and World
Wide Web. England had a rich theatrical heritage, not
only of the religious plays produced by civic guilds that
Shakespeare might have seen in his boyhood but also of
theatrical performances in the colleges at Oxford and
Cambridge and entertainments by players who, as members of noble households, regularly toured the countryside.

Theatre historians of the period have found a wealth
of evidence in private libraries, guildhalls, and public
record offices all over England of provincial performances

of all kinds. Shakespeare was born into a society that valued popular theatrical entertainment and celebrated many festive holidays with singing, dancing, and theatricals. Although touring and provincial playing were thus well known, the explosion of theatre construction and the formation of professional acting companies in London in the last two decades of the 16th century were unprecedented. The tremendous popularity of the new London playhouses represented a commercial and artistic opportunity that hindsight reveals to be perfectly suited to the expressive gifts of the talented and ambitious newcomer from Stratford.

CONCLUSION

*F*ellow playwright Ben Jonson concluded that Shakespeare "was not of an age, but for all time!" and time has thus far supported his bold declaration: no writer before or since has equaled Shakespeare in influence, reverential acclaim, or enduring commercial and popular success. Although his work has been studied more than that of any other writer, the facts of his life remain maddeningly elusive. Some skeptics still claim that the son of a Stratford glover could not possibly have written such an unparalleled body of work. And, in fact, the sort of uncritical reverence that Shakespeare often receives can lead to disappointment. The apocryphal first-time reader of *Hamlet* who comes away disgusted because the play turned out to be "nothing but quotes" testifies to the level of Shakespeare's saturation of our culture—and to the understandable impulse to mock and debunk so iconic a figure. Today, as we know, Shakespeare's works are performed all over the world in almost every language, including Klingon, and transferred to many historical periods and even some futuristic locations. They are produced in every imaginable medium, including comic books and pornographic travesties.

Indeed, Shakespeare's literary and cultural authority is now so unquestioned that it has taken on an aura of historical inevitability and has enshrined the figure of the solitary author as the standard-bearer of literary production. It is all the more important, then, to suggest that Shakespeare had a genius for timing—managing to be born in exactly the right place and at the right time to nourish his particular form of greatness. There can be no doubt that his birth occurred at a singularly propitious moment in the history of the English language, education, the theatre, and England's social and political world.

CHRONOLOGY OF THE
SHAKESPEAREAN WORLD, 1543–1700

*T*his chronology begins not with Shakespeare's birth (as might be expected) but, arbitrarily, with the death of the Polish astronomer Nicolaus Copernicus, whose much-maligned model of the solar system profoundly shifted human perception of the world and humanity's place in it. It ends with the closing of London's theatres.

1543

Polish astronomer Nicolaus Copernicus dies.

1547

Henry VIII, husband to six women and father of three monarchs, dies.
The reign of Edward VI begins.
Spanish writer Miguel de Cervantes is born.

1552/53

Edmund Spenser is born.

1553

The reign of Edward VI ends.
French writer François Rabelais dies.
The reign of Mary I begins.

1554

Sir Philip Sidney is born.

1555

Persecution of English Protestants begins, giving Mary I the nickname Bloody Mary.

1558

The reign of Mary I ends.
The reign of Elizabeth I begins.

1561

Francis Bacon is born.

1562

French Wars of Religion begin.
Spanish dramatist Lope de Vega is born.

1564

William Shakespeare is born.
Italian philosopher, astronomer, and mathematician Galileo is born.
Christopher Marlowe is born.

1572

John Donne is born.
Ben Jonson is born.

1576

The Theatre opens.

1577

Sir Francis Drake sets sail on his circumnavigation of the world.
Curtain Theatre opens.
Flemish painter Peter Paul Rubens is born.

1585

Sir Walter Raleigh is knighted.

1586

Sir Philip Sidney dies.

1587

Rose Theatre opens.
Mary, Queen of Scots, is executed.

1588

The Spanish Armada is routed.

1589

Geographer Richard Hakluyt's *Voyages* is published.

1589–93

Shakespeare's first several plays are produced.

1590

Edmund Spenser's *The Faerie Queene* is published.

1592

Thomas Kyd's *The Spanish Tragedie* is entered in the Stationers' Register.

1593

Christopher Marlowe is killed under mysterious circumstance.

1593–94

Shakespeare's first history plays—the three parts of *Henry VI*—are completed.

1595

Swan Theatre opens.

1596

Sir Francis Drake's last expedition, against the Spanish possessions in the West Indies, begins and ends, unsuccessfully.
French philosopher, mathematician, and scientist René Descartes is born.

1596–97

The Merchant of Venice and *Henry IV, Part 1*, are performed.

1597

Francis Bacon's *Essays* are published.

1597–98

Henry IV, Part 2, is published.

1599

The first Globe Theatre opens.
Edmund Spenser dies.
Henry V is performed.

1599–1601

Hamlet is performed.

1600

Fortune Theatre opens.
Spanish playwright and poet Pedro Calderón de la Barca
 is born.

1600–02

Twelfth Night is performed.

1603

The reign of Elizabeth I ends.
The reign of James I begins.

1603–04

Othello and *Measure for Measure* performed.

1605

The Gunpowder Plot is hatched.

1605–06

King Lear is performed.

1606

Dutch painter and printmaker Rembrandt van Rijn is born.

1607

The first permanent English settlement in North America,
 Jamestown (now in Virginia), is established.

1608

John Smith becomes president of Jamestown colony.
John Milton is born.

1609–11

The Winter's Tale is published.

1611

The King James Version of the Bible is published.
The Tempest is published.

1612–14

The Two Noble Kinsmen performed.

C. 1612

English-born American poet Anne Bradstreet (née Dudley) is born.

1613

Henry VIII and *Cardenio* (now lost), believed to be the original of *Double Falsehood*, are performed.
The first Globe Theatre burns down.

1616

William Shakespeare dies.
Miguel de Cervantes dies.

1617

The ascendancy of George Fillers, 1st duke of Buckingham, begins.

1618

The Thirty Years' War begins.

1619

A Dutch slaver delivers the first cargo of Africans to Virginia.

1620

The Pilgrims reach Plymouth and sign the Mayflower Compact.

1622

French playwright Molière is born.

1623

The First Folio is published.
French mathematician, physicist, and philosopher Blaise Pascal is born.

1625

The reign of James I ends.
The reign of Charles I begins.

1626

Dutchman Peter Minuit purchases the island of Manhattan (now the nucleus of New York City).
Francis Bacon dies.

1629

Charles I dissolves Parliament.

1631

John Donne dies.
John Dryden is born.

1632

Dutch colonial governor Peter Stuyvesant begins a career
with the Dutch West India Company.

1635

Lope de Vega dies.

1637

Ben Jonson dies.

1639

French poet Jean Racine is born.

1640

The artist Peter Paul Rubens dies.

1642

The English Civil Wars begin.
Galileo dies.
The London theatres are closed.

alderman A person governing a kingdom, district, or shire in the service of the king or queen.

armada A large fleet of warships.

bailiff An official employed by a British sheriff to serve writs, make arrests, and carry out executions.

borough A town or urban constituency in Great Britain that sends a representative to Parliament.

buccaneer An unscrupulous adventurer that attacks and plunders ships at sea; a pirate.

burgess A parliamentary representative of an English borough.

colossus A person who attains great physical size or great power.

dialect A regional variety of a single language distinguished from other regional varieties by features of vocabulary, grammar, and pronunciation.

dramatist One who writes dramas or plays.

enclosure In Elizabethan and Jacobean England, the practice of enclosing farmland with a hedge or fence to increase pasture lands for manorial lords.

epitaph A brief statement commemorating a deceased person or something past.

folio A large sheet of paper folded in such a way to make two leaves, or four pages, of a book or manuscript. By extension, the term also refers to the book made in such a fashion.

galleon A heavy, square-rigged sailing ship of the 15th to early 18th centuries used for war or commerce, especially by the Spanish.

gentry The upper or ruling class, also known as the aristocracy.

papist An uncomplimentary term referring to one who adheres to the teachings of the pope and the Roman Catholic church.

pastoral play A drama portraying the lives of country people, particularly shepherds, in an idealized way.

patron Someone who offers financial and/or moral support to an individual or cause.

peerage Belonging to one of five ranks in British society.

posthumous Referring to an action or occasion following the death of an individual.

privateer One who sails aboard a private ship that is armed and licensed to attack enemy ships.

proscenium arch The arch that encloses the opening in the proscenium wall (the part of a modern stage in front of the curtain) through which the spectator sees the stage.

quarto Refers to a manuscript printed on a piece of paper cut four from a sheet.

secular Relating to worldly or nonreligious matters.

shire An administrative subdivision of land, namely a county, in England.

vernacular Relating to the common form of language of a given group or class, as opposed to formal or literary language.

yeoman A person belonging to the class of freeholders (property owners) below the gentry in social rank.

Among modern editions of Shakespeare's works are Stanley Wells and Gary Taylor (eds.), *William Shakespeare, The Complete Works* , 2nd ed. (2005); G. Blakemore Evans and J.J. Tobin (eds.), *The Riverside Shakespeare*, 2nd ed. (1997); David Bevington (ed.), *The Complete Works of Shakespeare*, 6th ed. (2009); and Stephen Greenblatt (ed.), *The Norton Shakespeare* , 2nd ed. (2008). Three major scholarly series were in progress at the turn of the 21st century, with plays and poems in individual volumes: Stanley Wells (ed.), *The Oxford Shakespeare* (1982–); Philip Brockbank (ed.), *The New Cambridge Shakespeare* (1984–); and Richard Proudfoot, Ann Thompson, H.R. Woudhuysen, and David Scott Kastan (eds.), *The Arden Shakespeare*, 3rd series (1995–).

The following biographies are especially informative: S. Schoenbaum, *William Shakespeare: A Documentary Life* (1975), and *William Shakespeare: Records and Images* (1981); Richard Dutton, *William Shakespeare: A Literary Life* (1989); Dennis Kay, *Shakespeare: His Life, Work, and Era* (1992); Stanley Wells, *Shakespeare: A Life in Drama* (1995, reissued 1997); and Park Honan, *Shakespeare: A Life* (1998). Also useful is Stephen Greenblatt, *Will in the World: How Shakespeare Became Shakespeare* (2004). An excellent guide to any study of Shakespeare is Margreta De Grazia and Stanley Wells (eds.), *The New Cambridge Companion to Shakespeare*, 2nd ed. (2010). Shakespeare's language is the subject of David Crystal and Ben Crystal, *Shakespeare's Words: A Glossary and Language Companion* (2002); and Kenneth Gross, *Shakespeare's Noise* (2001). Also of note is Stanley Wells, *A Dictionary of Shakespeare* (2005).

Further information on Shakespeare's times can be gleaned from other biographies as well. Accessible biographies of Elizabeth include Alison Weir, *The Life of Elizabeth I* (1998); Anne Somerset, *Elizabeth I* (1991, reissued 2003); and Susan Doran, *Queen Elizabeth I* (2003). J.E. Neale, *Queen Elizabeth* (1934, reissued as *Queen Elizabeth I*, 1971), was long the standard biography. Supplementary scholarly biographies include J.B. Black, *The Reign of Elizabeth, 1558–1603*, 2nd ed. (1959); Neville Williams, *Elizabeth, Queen of England* (1967; U.S. title, *Elizabeth the First, Queen of England*, 1968), which stresses the formation under Elizabeth of an English national consciousness; and Paul Johnson, *Elizabeth I* (U.K. title, *Elizabeth I: A Study in Power and Intellect*, 1974). Jasper Ridley, *Elizabeth I* (1987; U.S. title, *Elizabeth I: The Shrewdness of Virtue*, 1988), emphasizes the role of religion in the queen's domestic and foreign policy. David Starkey, *Elizabeth: Apprenticeship* (2000), is a fresh look based on a rereading of her early life. Popular biographies of Elizabeth, even when well researched, tend to be highly speculative about Elizabeth's emotions and motivations. Among them are Carolly Erickson, *The First Elizabeth* (1983); and Alison Plowden, *The Young Elizabeth* (1971), and *Elizabeth Regina: The Age of Triumph, 1588–1603* (1980).

Books on theatre of Shakespeare's period are Richard Dutton, *The Oxford Handbook of Early Modern Theatre* (2009); Charles Whitney, *Early Responses to Renaissance Drama* (2006); Andrew Gurr, *Playgoing in Shakespeare's London*, 3rd ed. (2004); and Eric J. Griffin, *English Renaissance Drama and the Specter of Spain: Ethnopoetics and Empire* (2009).

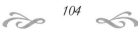